What peor

Pe.

Persephone: Practicing the Art ~, ... ersonal Power explores an often overlooked aspect of Pagan practice and life itself. We speak of Love and Light, but Persephone herself embodies Love and Darkness – finding her own power, seeking her deep truths, and so teaching others in turn. We all face challenges, but Persephone asks us to see them (and ourselves) from a new perspective. Like Her, you will return from this book changed, and definitely for the better. Please do seek it out.

Cat Treadwell, Druid Priest and author of *Facing the Darkness*

After we make our journey to the Underworld, our soul and human life forever straddle two worlds. We step into our power and reclaim personal sovereignty – the subject of this powerful book. The paradox is that we can bring things to light only by making the journey into the deepest darkness of the unknown, of death and dismemberment. Not just that, we must we commit to making this journey over and over if we are to continue peeling away the layers of our own shadow and unveil our authentic or true self. In *Persephone: Practicing the Art of Personal Power*, Robin Corak shows us the way as an initiate!

Imelda Almqvist, author of *Natural Born Shamans: A Spiritual Toolkit for Life* and *Sacred Art: Where Art Meets Shamanism*

Robin Corak has crafted a gem worthy of Persephone in all Her multi-faceted glory. Clearly informed by meticulous scholarship, this book is a thought-provoking foray into the myth of Persephone and the Eleusinian Mysteries, inviting the reader to gain greater self-awareness of his or her own movement beyond dependence and helplessness to empowerment and choice. Deceptively slim, there is a lot packed into *Persephone: Practicing the Art of Personal Power*. Presenting brilliant pathwork from Kore to Queen; the refreshing and deeply moving perspective of Persephone's tale told in Her own voice; and insightful journal questions, this book contains everything you need to open to a meaningful relationship both with the Goddess and with self. Particularly inspired and deeply relevant is Corak's weaving in the thread of Persephone's connection with the ancestors. At a time when there is as much focus on releasing ancestral karma as there is on healing personal trauma, this is an important and timely book. Alongside all the aspects of Persephone that make it a powerful guide to self-determination, there are ample practical suggestions for deepening a connection with this complex Goddess. The Discernment Divination, the rituals, and the list of correspondences are fantastic. And, in a book that is chock full of compelling reasons, the presentation of a feast (with recipes) to honour Persephone, is reason enough by itself to snap up this book. Whether you have worked with Persephone for years or are just coming to explore a relationship with this Goddess now, *Persephone: Practicing the Art of Personal Power* is a guide that highlights all the significant signposts and compelling stops along the journey. A book any psychopomp would be happy to call Hers.

Tiffany Lazic, author of *The Great Work: Self-Knowledge* and *Healing Through the Wheel of the Year*

Emerging from the Underworld and revealing Her glory both in Darkness and in Light, the mysteries of Persephone come alive in Robin Corak's fantastic addition to Moon Books' Pagan Portals series. Equal parts research and devotion, mythos and psychology, *Persephone: Practicing the Art of Personal Power* is as juicy as a pomegranate, and its yield is just as bountiful. A short volume by design, the book nevertheless delves deeply into Persephone's mythos, and lays out a full harvest of tools and workings for modern-day practitioners who wish to enter into relationship with Kore of the Flowering Spring, who is also Queen of the Underworld and a central figure in the Eleusinian Mysteries. A dazzling array of offerings can be found in these pages: ritual, divination, inner journeys, journaling prompts, and even instructions for putting together a ceremonial feast in honor of Persephone. There is something for everyone in this book, which will be of interest to long-standing devotees of Persephone as well as those feeling newly-called to work with this powerful Goddess who helps us to walk a path of empowerment.

Jhenah Telyndru, founder of the Sisterhood of Avalon and author of Pagan *Portals - Rhiannon: Great Queen of the Celtic Britons*

Pagan Portals

Persephone

Practicing the Art of Personal Power

Pagan Portals
Persephone

Practicing the Art of Personal Power

Robin Corak

MOON
BOOKS

Winchester, UK
Washington, USA

JOHN HUNT PUBLISHING

First published by Moon Books, 2020
Moon Books is an imprint of John Hunt Publishing Ltd., No. 3 East Street, Alresford
Hampshire SO24 9EE, UK
office@jhpbooks.net
www.johnhuntpublishing.com
www.moon-books.net

For distributor details and how to order please visit the 'Ordering' section on our website.

ISBN: 978 1 78904 333 4
978 1 78904 334 1 (ebook)
Library of Congress Control Number: 2019943840

A CIP catalogue record for this book is available from the British Library.

Design: Stuart Davies

UK: Printed and bound by CPI Group (UK) Ltd, Croydon, CR0 4YY
US: Printed and bound by Thomson-Shore, 7300 West Joy Road, Dexter, MI 48130

We operate a distinctive and ethical publishing philosophy in
all areas of our business, from our global network of authors to
production and worldwide distribution.

Contents

Acknowledgements

There are so many people who have contributed in some way to helping me write this book that I could not possibly name everyone. I will therefore do my best to hit the highlights, but know that if you have crossed my path in any meaningful way at some point in my life, I am grateful for the lessons you have taught me and the ways in which you have inspired me.

First and foremost, I would like to thank Trevor Greenfield and the Moon Books team for giving me the opportunity to bring this book to life. I am deeply grateful for your support!

My family has been an integral part of my ability and determination to live my life from a place of authenticity, strength, and courage. I have been fortunate enough to be surrounded by some truly amazing, inspiring, strong women including my mother; Sandi, my sister; Lisa, my nieces; O'Rian and Anam, and my stepdaughter, Emily. I am also fortunate to have a father, Bill, who always told me I could do anything I set my mind to. My brother-in-law, Jimmy, and my son-in-law, Barrett, are not intimidated by strong women and, in fact, are dedicated to helping the women in their life fulfill their dreams. I am grateful to have you in my life.

To my stepson, Steven Corak, you enact your personal power with an amazing combination of compassion, patience, and strength. I appreciate your contribution of the amazing recipes featured in Chapter 8 so very much. You are quite talented and the food you made for Persephone's feast aligned with my intent perfectly (not to mention that it was some of the best food I have ever eaten!)

I am thankful for my longtime friends, Jackie and Stephanie, who have been my cheerleaders in addition to being there for me whenever I needed to bounce ideas off of them or simply share my insecurities as an author. Benjamin, I thank you for believing in me and seeing the potential that existed in me long before I believed in or saw these things in myself. You encouraged me to shine and taught me that while the mountain may sometimes look like cardboard, it is truly built on a foundation of solid rock.

Vyviane, thank you for donating your time and energy to review my first book proposal and provide invaluable insights. Aidan, thank you for your willingness to share your insights and research.

I am immensely thankful for the Sisterhood of Avalon. My sisters and the wisdom and practices found in the SOA tradition have enriched my life beyond words. I am especially grateful for the wisdom and support of Jhenah and Tiffany as well as the encouragement of the SOA Board of Trustees and Council of Nine.

Finally, I wish to thank my husband, Richard, and my son, Owen. Owen, you have taught me so much about life and love and I am in awe of your enormous, empathic heart and your wise insights. You have cheered me on since day one and it means more than you know. Richard, my soulmate and best friend, you have truly taught me what it means to be loved unconditionally and as a result I have learned to love myself more deeply as well. Thank you for always believing in me, supporting me, and encouraging me to practice the art of personal power. You are my sanctuary, my home, and my heart and I couldn't have done this without you. I love you.

Introduction

With my hands touching the remnants of a large marble column, I stood in the glaring heat atop a platform of stone and surveyed the scene laid out before me. I was finally here, in Eleusis, the location of the Eleusinian Mysteries and the site sacred to the goddess Persephone. I could feel her presence near and could hear her voice in my mind, welcoming me. The journey here had been a lengthy one, both physically and symbolically.

As a child, I was diagnosed with a rare medical condition and my family and friends did everything that they could for me in order to overcompensate for my fragile state. My condition, paired with a paralyzing shyness, left me feeling weak and incapable of making decisions for myself. The concept of personal power was foreign to me. My sanctuary was my room, where I lost myself in innumerable stories and myths.

It was during this time that I first came across the story of Persephone and I was both drawn to her and bewildered by her. Here was a young girl who, much like me, appeared to not be able to choose for herself. As she was out picking flowers one day, the ground suddenly opened up and Hades abducted Persephone and took her to the Underworld. Her mother, Demeter, had previously declined offers of marriage for Persephone from two other gods and had moved her to a more isolated place in an effort to protect her daughter and her innocence. Her father, Zeus, had actually conspired with Hades in her abduction, thinking that Persephone would be a good marital match for his brother. Both her mother and father felt that they knew what was best for her and in an effort to perhaps shield her or ensure her life was a happy, successful one (by their definition of course), they did not grant her the independence that she both needed and deserved.

It seemed to me that Persephone herself did not have the

ability or willingness to challenge her role as a helpless pawn. On the one hand, I was excited to resonate so strongly with a deity. I hadn't previously encountered a story wherein a character who was described as having a powerful title such as "goddess" or "queen" shared the same struggles that I did. Conversely, I was also baffled by the very fact that Persephone was a goddess and yet she didn't seem to have any control over her own life let alone the lives of others. I initially vacillated between being inspired at having found a deity that I shared so much in common with and being distraught, because if a goddess couldn't figure out how to run her own life, what chance did I have?

I didn't realize at the time that had I explored Persephone's myth further, I would have found the answers to my questions.

Persephone continued to fascinate me, both as a character in myth and when I began my exploration into Paganism. Over time, as the people around me finally realized that I needed to learn to be independent and as I began to fight for my own autonomy, I was able to see Persephone in a new light. For while it may seem on the surface that Persephone is the helpless maiden torn between the controlling forces in her life, if we dig a bit deeper we can see that Persephone is truly the embodiment of sovereignty. She teaches us about discernment, choice, authenticity, and personal power. She guides us through the shadowy realms of our subconscious to face our demons and fears so that we might rise again in the light of our personal power and potential and claim that which we desire.

Revisiting Persephone's myth as I grew older and being able to better understand the underlying themes in her story helped me tremendously in my efforts to build confidence, understand my own strength, and act from a place of self-knowledge and self-determination. While I have gone on to explore other deities over the past 20 years, Persephone has never truly left my side and her presence and guidance have certainly had a powerful impact. Today I am the CEO of a large, social services organization with a consolidated budget of $66 million and hundreds of employees and volunteers. I have won awards, taught leadership development to youth and adults, and regularly give compelling speeches to crowds of hundreds.

While I was fortunate enough to have live mentors that helped me along the way, it was goddesses such as Persephone who first provided the spark that I needed to see myself in a different light and whom inspired me to move from that place of powerless maiden to sovereign woman. We live in a society where basic rights for some sectors of the community are being threatened and where there are increasing efforts to make choices for women without their input or representation. What better time to invoke the lessons and attributes of a goddess who not only has fought successfully for control over her own fate but who - as Queen of both the Underworld and Spring - also has the ability to cut ties with that which no longer serves her and manifest that which does?

As you undertake the journey with Persephone that unveils throughout the next nine chapters, it is important to know what we are striving for when we work with Persephone. Therefore, it is critical to take a look at what personal power is and isn't. Often times, we may perceive personal power as exercising our authority over others and/or persuading someone to accept and agree with our views. The concept of personal power can be particularly challenging at times for those of us who have experienced trauma in our childhood or who have not been exposed to a healthy modeling of personal power. Going from having no concept of personal power to finally speaking our truth and enacting our beliefs and visions can be a heady, overwhelming experience which can sometimes end up being very painful and disheartening.

Personal power is much more subtle than one might initially expect. There are no dramatics to announce that we are moving into our own sovereignty and those around us might not notice the shift at first. Yet it is a very impactful shift nonetheless. Personal sovereignty is not concerned with formal titles and positions of authority, though it is certainly not uncommon for those who have manifested their personal power to act in formal leadership positions. Sovereignty is not about controlling others, nor is it about using one's voice and strength to silence other voices, particularly those that express opinions that are not in alignment with our own. Being sovereign is an act of self-determination; choosing for ourselves from a place of conscious intent rather than reacting based on patterns, fears, and/or beliefs that have not been brought to light.

Working with Persephone requires complete self-honesty and self-accountability. Persephone requires that we be willing to be vulnerable if we are to realize our potential and access the sovereignty that lies within each and every one of us. She teaches us that we do have choices - however limited they may sometimes seem. Persephone helps us to understand that while we may not have the ability to change events that impact us, we do have the ability to choose how we react to those events.

Unearthing our own inner "Persephone" does not happen overnight, nor is it a strictly linear process. Just as Persephone descends to the Underworld and ascends back to Earth each year, so too, must we commit to undertaking this journey on an ongoing basis if we are to peel away the layers of our own shadow and fulfill the potential of our higher self. The self-sovereignty that we access as a result of working with Persephone provides us with the ability to identify and make choices through the lens of what we most deeply desire and hold dear. By embracing our own power, we also give permission to those around us to do so as well.

This book integrates research, storytelling and hands on techniques to help you connect deeply with Persephone, her story, and her lessons. Chapters One and Two provide foundational information about the various versions of Persephone's myth as well as what we know about the Eleusinian Mysteries; highly secretive rites which were enacted in honor of Persephone and her mother, Demeter, each year in ancient Greece. The remaining chapters look at how we might work with Persephone and incorporate her wisdom into our own lives. All chapters contain thought provoking journal questions and/or hands on activities to help you work and deeply connect with Persephone, access your own inner wisdom, build your confidence, and claim your personal power.

It is my sincere hope that the information and tools provided throughout this book will allow you to find in Persephone a strong guide, teacher, and role model, helping you to embrace and unleash the divinity that resides within you.

Chapter 1

From Helpless Child to Powerful Woman

Persephone is not one of the Olympians in the Greek pantheon yet her myth is familiar to many and is often taught as part of school curriculums. Known as Proserpina in Rome, Persephone was worshipped in two ways, almost as if she had a split personality. The first aspect of Persephone was the "Kore"; the beautiful young and innocent maiden who was associated with spring. Kore means "girl" or "maiden" in Greek and there are innumerable statues and sculptures of Kore throughout Greece. As her story progresses, she becomes the "Queen of the Underworld", a mature goddess who reigns over the dead and guides the living who visit the Underworld.

Perhaps the most well-known version of Persephone's story comes to us from the Homeric hymn entitled, "Hymn to Demeter". One of several poems composed by different and sometimes unknown authors from the 8th century B.C. to the Hellenistic period, the "Hymn to Demeter" provides the earliest glimpse of the Eleusinian rites and Demeter's cult. Unfortunately, we do not know which author composed "Hymn to Demeter", but we do know that it was likely written sometime in the 7th century BC (Shelmerdine, 1995). While the hymn focuses primarily on Persephone's mother, Demeter, it describes Hades' abduction of Persephone and the roles other gods and goddesses play in trying to assuage Demeter's subsequent depression.

In the traditional telling of Persephone's story, she is out picking flowers one day when she is drawn to a narcissus flower. As she approaches the flower, a hole suddenly opens up in the ground and Hades emerges from the chasm with his chariot. He kidnaps the frightened Persephone and takes her off to the Underworld to be his bride. When Demeter learns of her daughter's disappearance, she becomes distraught and immediately sets off to find her. Line 47 in the "Hymn to Demeter" states,

> "For nine days, then, over the earth queenly Deo
> roamed about, holding blazing torches in her hands" (Shelmerdine, 1995, 36)

During this time, Demeter refuses to eat, drink or bathe. The goddess Hecate arrives with her own torch and informs Demeter that her daughter was abducted, but Hecate does not know the identity of her kidnapper. The god Helios then tells Demeter that it was Hades who took her daughter but that she should not worry as he believes Hades will be a good husband for Persephone. This only infuriates Demeter, and she vows to not visit Olympus and to not let anything grow on Earth until she is reunited with her daughter.

Demeter wanders until she arrives at the house of Keleos, lord of Eleusis, and sits grieving by a well. The daughters of Keleos see her in her human guise and suggest that she come to their house. No one in the house of Keleos initially suspects that the woman standing before them is a goddess. Demeter refuses the chair that is offered to her by the Queen Metaneira as well as the food offered to her by a woman named Iambe (sometimes known as Baubo in alternate versions of the story). Iambe is able to distract her from her grief:

> "Until devoted Iambe, intervening with jokes
> and many jests, moved the holy lady
> to smile and laugh and have a propitious heart,
> indeed in later times too she used to please her in her moods"
> (Shelmerdine, 1995, 44)

Although Iambe plays a minor role in the hymn, her attempts

to amuse Demeter were re-enacted as a standard part of the Eleusinian Mysteries. The hymn then branches off into Demeter acting as a nursemaid for Metaneira's son. While this piece of the story isn't as relevant to Persephone's fate, it does play a crucial role in describing how the temple to Demeter and the Eleusinian Mysteries were established.

Throughout this time, Demeter's depression has caused a famine on Earth. Zeus recognizes that if Demeter were allowed to continue this way, she would soon wipe out the human race. Of course, Zeus' concerns were not entirely unselfish as he realized that without humans the Greek gods and goddesses would not have anyone to worship them and offer gifts and sacrifices. Zeus sends a string of gods and goddesses to plead with Demeter and offer her gifts but she insists that she will not return to Olympus and return the Earth to its normal state until she sees her daughter again with her own eyes.

At Zeus' request, the god Hermes travels down to the Underworld to explain to Hades that Demeter has sunk into a deep depression which has caused the Earth to become barren and therefore threatens humanity. Hermes tells Hades that Zeus has ordered that Persephone be reunited with her mother so that the Earth can once again flourish. Despite Hades' avowals that Persephone will be a powerful queen and goddess if she stays in the Underworld with him, Persephone jumps at the chance to leave. In Homer's version of Persephone's tale, Hades forcefully slips pomegranate seeds into Persephone's mouth, knowing that if she consumes any food while in his realm, she will be forced to return to the Underworld.

Persephone is reunited with her mother, and while Demeter is overjoyed to be with her daughter again, she suspects something is wrong. Demeter asks Persephone if she consumed any food while in the Underworld. Persephone swears to tell the truth and states:

"...But Hades secretly
put in my mouth the seed of a pomegranate, honey-sweet food,
and, though I was unwilling, he made me eat it by force."
(Shelmerdine, 1995, 55)

Because she had consumed food while in the Otherworld, Persephone was fated to remain in the Underworld one-third of the year and would get to spend the other two-thirds of the year with her mother at the onset of spring. Zeus sent Demeter's mother, Rhea, to lead her back to Olympus and Demeter immediately restored the Earth's fertility.

In the Homeric "Hymn to Demeter", it is apparent that Persephone is portrayed as an innocent maiden with no control over her own destiny. Her mother wishes to keep her innocent and by her side, even refusing two offers for Persephone's hand in marriage from the powerful gods Apollo and Hermes without ever consulting her daughter. Persephone's father, Zeus, assumes he knows what is best for her and conspires with his brother so that Hades may abduct her. Hades forces Persephone to go with him and be his wife.

Worse yet, Hades forces himself on Persephone. Zeus later controls his daughter's fate once again by having Hermes take her back to her mother and yet again by sentencing her to live part of her life in the Underworld as a result of her having eaten seeds which Hades forced her to eat. Even Gaia, the beloved Earth goddess and great-grandmother to Persephone, is said to aid in the abduction! Gaia's betrayal is evident in line eight of the hymn which states, "...and the narcissus which Gaia made grow as a trick for the blushing maiden" (Shelmerdine, 1995). Clearly, in this hymn, Persephone is a victim, subject to the whims of others in her life who make decisions for her. She is portrayed as weak, dependent, and unable to direct her own fate. Yet, this is not all there is to Persephone's myth.

What if Persephone was not the victim but rather the victor?

Other versions of Persephone's myth written by authors such as Orpheus and Musaeus show a much different perspective of Persephone. The Orphic hymns make no mention of Persephone being abducted or raped nor does there appear to be any evidence in the art of Demeter's Eleusinian temple that illustrate that a rape took place (Reif, 1999). It is therefore unlikely that the rape aspect of the Homeric hymn came from Eleusis. In addition, we know that the Eleusinian Mysteries included some sort of re-enactment of Persephone's abduction. Because initiates were sworn to secrecy, the author of the "Hymn to Demeter" could not have portrayed the myth exactly as it was shared in the rites of the Mysteries.

It is important to also keep in mind that the works by Homeric authors and other authors such as Ovid were written in patriarchal times and this was bound to influence the way in which the Greek myths were told. Author Charlene Spretnak asserts that the Greek myths began to include subjects of rape and men asserting dominance over women when Greece transitioned from a matriarchal to a patriarchal society (Spretnak, 1992). Exploration of cultural factors uncovers a tradition in Greek marriage ceremonies in which a mock abduction of the bride was enacted and it is therefore possible that this tradition is reflected - albeit in a literal way - in the Homeric hymn. Goddesses such as Persephone, Hera and Aphrodite were of great significance to brides and worship of these goddesses was incorporated into the pre-wedding rituals (Parca, 2007). For the ancient Greeks, the story of Hades' abduction of Persephone "...represented the vulnerability of the young woman during her perilous journey to womanhood, which girls were expected to make through marriage." (Tzanetou, 2007).

The transition from child to woman is inherent in Persephone's story if we look at it from a deeper symbolic level. Persephone is an innocent young maiden, poised on the precipice of womanhood. We typically don't make the leap from child to adult in one fell swoop; rather, there is often a sustained period in which we exist within the chasm between the two. The maturation process is like a slow death, as we must shed our innocence and dependency. As we grow into our independence, information which we may have been shielded from before is revealed and we are made aware of things that threaten to shatter our feelings of security. We are no longer allowed the luxury of being carefree as we must now make our own decisions and be accountable for our own actions. Metaphorically, being plunged into darkness when we have spent most of our lives in the light is terrifying.

With some exceptions, most of us have the ability to ease into our adulthood and traverse back and forth between the worlds of childhood and adulthood before having to make the final transition. Yet, Persephone (at least in the Homeric hymn), does not have this option. She is, without warning, taken from the light and from everything she knows and thrown into the darkness and the unknown. Those of us who did not have the fortune to ease out of childhood due to situations such as abuse, lack of a stable home, and/or other traumatic events can often relate to this aspect of Persephone's story. While Persephone experiences a descent into a literal Underworld, so too does the process of growth plunge us into our own spiritual and emotional Underworld. This is an experience that we must all go through at some point and we often repeat the cycle of descent and ascent in various ways throughout our lives.

Despite the fear that a descent into the Underworld can provoke, there is also deep wisdom and power to be found in this shadowy realm. It has been suggested that during the time of matriarchies, women were perceived to hold deep and mysterious powers that allowed them and perhaps even guided them to access the Underworld (Reif, 1999). It may be that this perception contributed to the decline in societies revering rather than fearing women. Descending into the Underworld and doing the work required to confront our shadows to ultimately emerge into the light grants one a unique power, wisdom and even a sense of freedom.

It is interesting to note that Hecate, a Greek goddess also associated with the Underworld, becomes Persephone's attendant and constant companion towards the end of her story. A powerful and magical deity, Hecate is often viewed as a crone goddess. Crone goddesses are typically thought to be very wise, having fought life's battles and accumulated knowledge as a result of their vast life experiences. One could view Hecate's alignment with Persephone as a symbolic reference to the wisdom that one attains as result of the challenges that accompany personal growth.

If we look at Persephone's story from a perspective of empowerment, we can see that Persephone is far from being a victim. While it is clear that she does experience trepidation and perhaps even resistance to marrying Hades and living in another realm, she ultimately comes into her own and goes after what she wants. Persephone's freedom and sovereignty appear to be limited by the choices imposed upon her by others. It would seem that she only has two options: either stay with Hades and grow into her own power but never see her mother again or return to her mother and be deprived of Hades' love and the opportunity to grow. But Persephone does not allow herself to be limited by what appear to be very rigid, limited options, both of which require a huge sacrifice. Persephone embraces her sovereignty and uses discernment to find a third way. Rather than being forced to eat the pomegranate seeds, Persephone chooses to do so knowing very well what the consequences will be. By choosing this path, Persephone must compromise to a degree but she is able to spend time with both of the people she loves and is granted the opportunity to flourish in the light as well as find and enact her personal power in the dark.

Other stories about Persephone are perhaps not as well

known, but it is interesting to note that these stories tend to show Persephone in a position of authority and/or as acting from a place of self-determination. In the Odyssey, Ulysses visits the Underworld and Persephone as its acting queen introduces Ulysses to the souls of famous women throughout history. In the myth of Psyche and Eros, Psyche's last task is to go to the Underworld with a box and request that Persephone fill it with a potion that will grant Aphrodite even more beauty. The last of Hercules' tasks was to get Persephone's permission to borrow Hades' three-headed dog Cerberus.

Finally, the story of Adonis provides an ironic twist. Having fallen in love with Adonis and fearing for his life because of her husband's jealousy, Aphrodite hides Adonis in a chest and sends him to Persephone with a request that she keep him safe. Persephone opens the chest and falls in love with Adonis, ultimately refusing to return him to Aphrodite. She fights with another deity for Adonis just as her mother fought with Hades for her.

Zeus is brought in to mediate the dispute and decides that Adonis should spend one third of the year with Persephone, one third of the year with Aphrodite, and the remaining third on his own. The heady and novel experience of embracing our personal power for the first time can tempt us to exert our power in a way that - intentionally or not - conflicts with another person's own sovereignty. This last story about Persephone and Adonis may act as a cautionary tale to remind us that sovereignty is power over self rather than power over others.

Oddly, despite initially being portrayed by Homer as an impotent character, Persephone was one of the most important goddesses in ancient Greek culture due to the Eleusinian Mysteries. These Mysteries, which will be explored in the next chapter, had an incredible influence not only on its initiates but on society and politics as well.

Persephone's Story-Reclaimed

Below is a reclaiming and retelling of Persephone's myth from her perspective and with a theme of empowerment.

The first time I saw him, I remember being surprised that there could be such beauty to be found in darkness. He was breathtaking.

I had been playing with the daughters of Okeanos and Tythos, picking flowers and laughing with my friends. It was one of the rare times that I was free to do as I wished; perhaps because the meadow was one of the few places that my mother, Demeter, felt was safe. My mother's desire to keep me near her hadn't bothered me when I was a young child, but now that I was on the precipice of womanhood I found it...suffocating. I loved my mother but I was also tired of being treated like a child. Whenever I tried to talk with her about things like my future or marriage, I could see the fear arise in her eyes and she would change the subject.

I had heard through the grapevine that two powerful Olympians - Apollo and Hermes - had asked my mother for my hand in marriage and she had turned them down without ever asking me what I thought. This infuriated me, but not because I wanted to marry them. Although, attractive as they were I could certainly have done worse! No, I was enraged because she did not think me capable of making my own decisions. I bottled up my anger as I always did, afraid to even broach the subject with my mother.

That day in the meadow, surrounded by lilies and roses, I glimpsed a flower off in the distance that seemed to have an otherworldly beauty. I wandered away from my friends, determined to get closer to this flower that seemed to glow. I bent down in front of it, admiring its golden inner circle surrounded by flowers as white as snow. Just as I reached out my hand to take possession of the narcissus, the ground shook and rumbled until, finally, a golden chariot emerged from the ground with a tall man with long dark hair at its helm. Shaking, I stood, and before I could protest, the man had grabbed me and descended back into the earth.

I screamed and screamed to no avail. Looking back, if I am honest with myself, I screamed because it was the natural thing to do. It was what would be expected of a maiden who had been abducted. The truth was that while I *was* scared and confused, I instinctively knew that the man's intent was not to harm me and for some odd reason I was drawn to him and to the possibility of seeing a land outside of my mother's domain.

Of course, I didn't let any of this show. We arrived in what appeared to be the Underworld and my captor introduced himself as the god Hades. At first, I was in shock. I did what I had always done when I was upset; I became quiet, and my eyes turned to ice. Hades explained that he was enchanted by me and that he wished to make me his wife. He said he was lonely, and that he desperately wanted someone to rule by his side in the Underworld. He added that while he had great respect for my mother, both he and my father, Zeus, had agreed that it was time for me to grow up and live my own life.

Anger erupted in me when he made this last statement. I don't think I had ever before allowed myself to truly feel my own anger and it was both exhilarating and terrifying. I didn't know why I suddenly had the courage to express the volcanic rage that was growing inside me, but I knew that I couldn't bottle it back up as I had done in the past. I yelled at him, calling him a bully, calling him weak, calling him a fool. I pointed out the irony that he would justify taking me without my permission by stating that he thought it was time that I live my own life and therefore make my own choices. With one last angry burst, I pushed him as hard as I could.

Of course, wall of muscle that he was, he didn't move. Yet, I could see the astonishment in his eyes which I am sure mirrored my own, and I ran. I ran down a maze of hallways in Hades' palace, until finally, finding a small room, I fell in a heap on the bed, exhausted. Hades found me later. I was prepared for a fight. I was prepared to try and run away. Surprisingly, he simply gave me a tender look and left me to my solitude.

Each day, the pain of missing my mother enveloped me to the point that I sometimes felt that I could not breathe. Yet over time, the tension between Hades and I dissolved and I began to better appreciate him. Despite having heard stories in my youth that painted him as a terrifying, hulking beast who had ill intentions and punished the dead, I found him to be a gentle, thoughtful creature. Moody, yes, but also able to pick up on my moods without a word being said. I found myself stimulated by our conversations - grown up conversations that my mother and my friends were never willing to have with me. I laughed at his stories and when I shared with him that I desperately missed my mother, he simply listened.

The first time he asked me what I thought, I said nothing. I didn't know what to think or what to say. I struggled to try and figure out which answer would most please him. When he inquired about my silence and asked again about my thoughts, I provided what I felt was the safest, least contradictory answer. Hades was quiet for a moment, and with a scornful look he admonished me.

He told me that I was no longer a child, and it was time I started acting like a woman. I began to speak but before I could say anything, he silenced me, telling me that a true Queen of the Underworld has her own thoughts and opinions and has no qualms about sharing them. I was too shocked to respond. He began to walk away but before he left the room he turned back and said quietly, "You would do well to not speak unless you are willing to be honest about what is in your mind and your heart. The next time you share a thought or give me an answer, you must be willing to own your words".

Day by day, my confidence grew and I began to cherish

the time that Hades and I spent together. In part because I was growing to love him and in part because he provided me with a freedom I had never before experienced. I still missed my mother terribly and felt guilty at times for taking even the slightest enjoyment or comfort from my time with Hades. At the same time, Hades helped me to better know and trust myself and encouraged me to step into my own personal power and this was a gift unlike any other I had ever received. Although initially most of our time was spent in the rooms of the palace, he soon began taking me to visit the parts of the Underworld that I had not seen.

At first, it was overwhelming seeing so many souls and absorbing so many feelings. My heart ached for the poor lost souls that wandered the realm because they had nothing to offer Chiron for transport across the river Acheron. I cried for the living who tried to gain entrance in order to reunite with their deceased loved ones-many of whom either could no longer be found or would not remember who they were. The Underworld was a cold, dark, dank place and I could understand why the living feared it as they did.

Hades found me crying one day and with a look of concern, he lovingly put his arm around me and asked me what the matter was. I told him of my sadness for the Underworld's inhabitants who were lost with no one to guide them. I cried for the living that were left behind, unable to let go of their loved ones and their pain for fear that their loved ones were in a bad place. I admonished him for creating such a depressing environment and bemoaned death's scythe.

Hades took me into his arms and told me that death was a very necessary albeit underappreciated part of nature's cycle. "Life", he said, "changes constantly like a river. We must let go again and again in order to live. Whether it's an aspect of ourselves, a person, a belief or a life that must die, it is necessary for us to release the past and shed our skin so that we may embrace life and be born again." As for the way the Underworld looked and the lost wanderings of the souls, with a gleam in his eye he said, "A Queen has the power to make changes in her own realm, does she not?"

Time went by and I threw myself into my work. At first, this was enough to dispel some of the pain that I felt at being separated from my mother and all I had known. More and more, however, as much as I loved being with Hades, I missed my mother with equal measure. Finally the day came when Hermes came to speak with Hades and me. He told us that in my mother's grief, she had caused a famine on Earth which threatened humanity. Zeus, he said, had ordered that I be reunited with my mother immediately to avert this disaster. Hades, dumbfounded, asked to be left alone with me for a few moments and Hermes acquiesced.

Hades led me to a courtyard where pomegranates had somehow managed to thrive. With great sorrow in his eyes, Hades took both of my hands and faced me. He told me that he understood my desire to reconcile with my mother and knew that he could never fill the void that the loss of being with her had created. However, he said, if I would only stay with him and rule by his side as a Queen, I would be a goddess, given the greatest honors among the immortals. He pleaded with me to defy my father's request and stay with him, and then left me alone to consider what I would do.

I had two paths before me, or so it seemed. Both allowed me to spend time alongside one I loved deeply but required that I sacrifice the other. Both paths had been presented to me as though I had no other options. The thought of returning to the light of the Earth and Olympus and being reunited with my mother filled me with joy, but the thought of leaving behind the man who had expanded my horizons, who viewed me as a capable woman and encouraged me to manifest my own power tore my heart in two. The same was true in reverse, for as much as

I loved Hades, how could I agree to live forever in the darkness, never to see my mother again?

Adrenaline pounded through me as I bowed me head and let the tears flow freely. I knew I was running out of time but I also knew that I simply could not accept either path laid before me. There had to be another way, and I was determined to find it. I looked up and immediately spied a ripe pomegranate, red as blood. I recalled being told as a child that if one ate anything while in the Underworld, he or she would be condemned to remain there forever. But given the seriousness of the Earth's condition, would Zeus truly risk the only people he had to worship him and the other gods by condemning me to a lifetime of living in the Underworld without reprieve? There was no time for me to ponder the answer to that question and so, without another moment to spare, I grabbed for the pomegranate. I tore it open, and slipped a few of the juicy crimson seeds under my tongue.

I then left the garden just as Hermes had come looking for me. With one last long look, I embraced Hades and climbed into Hermes' chariot without looking back. As soon as Hermes' chariot emerged from the ground, my mother ran to me, tears streaming down her face, and enveloped me in her arms. My heart soared and I felt a long lost comfort as she held me to her. After a few moments, she stepped back and suddenly frowned as though she sensed something was wrong.

"My dearest daughter", she said softly, "I am worried that perhaps you have been tricked by the devious brother of your father. Did you eat anything while in the Underworld, for if so, it is said that you will have to remain there forever."

Seeing the hurt and concern in her eyes, my initial reaction was to lie and tell her that Hades had forced me to eat the seeds to avoid her displeasure and disappointment in me. But my time in the Underworld had irrevocably changed me. Whereas I still maintained the light, carefree energy of my youth, I was now a woman-fully able and prepared to speak with honesty and determine my own fate. I admitted that shortly before my departure, I had eaten a few pomegranate seeds from the Underworld garden.

My mother gasped and the other gods and goddesses groaned. Zeus had been in attendance for our reunion, and a frustrated expression stole over his face. It would have been quite comical if he hadn't been so somber.

"This", Zeus said, shaking his head, "is no good. For if I send you back to the Underworld as is the custom and the law then humanity will perish and that will be disastrous for all of us."

Before Zeus could continue, I spoke up. "I certainly see your dilemma and have no intention in remaining in one place or the other. Is there any reason that I can't spend time in both realms?"

Zeus considered this possibility for a long moment, and then in a stance of authority, nodded. "Persephone, I decree that from this point forward you will spend part of the year with your mother on Earth and in Olympus and part of the year with your husband, Hades, in the Underworld."

I had found a third way that did not require me to fully sacrifice both of the people I loved. More importantly, I found my own way, taking control of my destiny with a strength and courage I had once thought I did not possess. To this day, I spend part of my time in the Underworld, acting as a sovereign psychopomp; guiding others through the dark, be it the dark of death's physical realm or the dark of one's shadowy subconscious. As the flowers begin to bloom on Earth, I spend the other part of my time sharing my abundance with others, showing them what could be and helping them to nurture the seeds of beauty, divinity, and power that reside in us all.

Journal Questions

- What aspects of Persephone's traditional stories most resonate with you? What aspects do you find the most challenging to understand or embrace? Why do you think these aspects resonate with you and/or challenging to understand or embrace?

- Are there aspects of the reclaimed story that resonate with you? If so, what and why? Are there aspects of the reclaimed story that don't resonate with you and, if so, why?

- In what ways have your life experiences paralleled Persephone's on a metaphorical level?

- Think about your own transition from child to adult. Did this happen over a period of time or was it something that happened with little warning and/or before you were ready for it? What impact do you think these experiences had on how you view yourself, your own power (or lack thereof) and the world around you?

- In what areas of your life do you find it easiest to speak your truth and act from a place of power? In what areas of your life do you find this to be challenging?

- Think about your own cultural heritage. How are girls viewed in your culture? Are there any traditions that marked or celebrated the rite of passage from your being a girl to becoming a woman? What impact do you think these rites might have had (positive and/or negative) on how you view your own power?

- What parts of your own story do you feel need to be reclaimed? How might you retell them?

- What does sovereignty mean to you? If you were your most sovereign self, what would that look like?

Chapter 2

The Eleusinian Mysteries

The religious rites known as the Eleusinian Mysteries were carried out by the cult of Demeter, which is believed by some to be the oldest mystery cult (Stehle, 2007). Many mystery rites and traditions have since used the Eleusinian Mysteries as their model and foundation. Powerful people - including emperors and philosophers - were initiated into the Eleusinian Mysteries (Uzzell, 2017). Interestingly, the Mysteries were both secretive and state sponsored (Stehle, 2007). Due to their accessibility, the Mysteries worked to bring ancient Greek society together as anyone could be initiated so long as they were a Greek citizen and were of sound morals and had not committed crimes such as murder. There is evidence to indicate that Greek speaking foreigners could also participate in the Mysteries (Shelmerdine, 1995). Age, gender, and social class did not pose any barrier to participating in the rites.

Eleusis, the location where the rites were carried out, is a small town roughly 14 miles from Athens. The name "Eleusis" means "place of happy arrival" and its mysteries were already centuries old by the 1st century BC (Reif, 1999). Much like the Temple of Delphi, the site of Eleusis featured multiple Greek gods and goddesses which changed over time. Greek deities such as Hecate, Artemis, and Poseidon had a presence at Eleusis at varying times alongside Demeter, Persephone and Plouton (previously known as Hades).

Many historians have asserted that the Eleusinian Mysteries were heavily influenced by the Thesmophoria; a secretive women's ritual dedicated to Demeter (Stehle, 2007). Much like the Eleusinian rites, the Thesmophoria contained themes of both agricultural cycles and the human cycle of death and rebirth. Despite the fact that women did not hold much power in Greek society, they took center stage as catalysts and participants in the Thesmophoric and Eleusinian rituals. The combination of womens' roles in these types of religious rites and the reverence that the patriarchal society held for the Eleusinian Mysteries ensured that the stories of Persephone and Demeter and the women who brought them to life were certain to have a strong influence on Greek society at that time as well as on the history of Greek religion.

The Homeric "Hymn to Demeter" introduces us to the concept of the Eleusinian Mysteries and Demeter's cult via Demeter's request to have a temple dedicated to her in Eleusis. At the time that the hymn was written, Demeter's cult kept within the confines of Eleusis and was overseen by families who passed down the responsibility of the Mysteries from generation to generation (Uzzell, 2017). While Eleusis was initially an independent city-state, the city and the Mysteries were greatly influenced by other geographic areas and events. At the end of the Mycenaean period, Greece experienced a famine which threatened its inhabitants. As was common for the time, the Oracle of Delphi was consulted in an effort to determine how to stop the famine. The prophecy that was given instructed that a festival and sacrifice should be dedicated to Eleusis each year in honor of Demeter and that this would end the famine (Preka-Alexandri, 1997).

By the 6th century BC, Eleusis came under the control of Athens and it is this event which ultimately led to the sacred procession from Athens to Eleusis as a critical piece of the Mystery rites (Uzzell, 2017). Both Eleusis and Athens benefitted from this change in power as the sacred procession brought notoriety to both cities as well as economic growth. Each year, Athens would send the first fruits of its harvest to Eleusis and would appoint a child to undergo initiation in the upcoming rites to ensure abundance and blessings (Uzzell, 2017). Due to the secretive nature of the Mysteries, we cannot know for certain in detail what occurred. However, historical research as well as archeological evidence can provide some clues and insights.

There were two components to the Eleusinian Mysteries - the Lesser Mysteries and the Greater Mysteries. Initiation only occurred once someone had first completed the rites of the Lesser Mysteries. The Lesser Mysteries were held in Agra (a suburb of Athens) and took place in the month we know as February, seven months before the Greater Mysteries would begin (Shelmerdine, 1995; Preka-Alexandri, 1997). These mysteries had a primary theme of ritual purification. Initiates had to swear to keep the Mysteries a secret, and any violation of this oath could be punishable by law with potential consequences including but not limited to exile.

There was a large cast of characters that helped to perform the rites. These included, but were not limited to, priestesses of Demeter and Persephone, various other priests and priestesses, and a Hierophant. The vast majority of clergy for the Mysteries were selected from families who had originally come from Eleusis and/or had long owned property there. In most cases, the sacred titles were passed down from generation to generation.

The Greater Mysteries took place in the season that we commonly refer to as Autumn (September/October), and were said to last nine days in honor of the nine days Demeter spent wandering in search of her daughter. First time participants of the mysteries were referred to as "Mystai" (Shelmerdine, 1995). They were accompanied by "Epoptai"; those who had already participated in the rites and were viewed as "watchers" or "those who have seen" (Shelmerdine, 1995; Uzzell, 2017). The role of the Epoptai was to help guide and support the Mystai through their initiation.

The timing of the Greater Mysteries was aligned with the first harvests. As author Jennifer Reif states:

"The mysteries occur at the end of the fallow period, before the fall rains. This is a pivotal time between the barren and fertile periods of the yearly cycle." (Reif, 1999, 218)

Certainly seasonal agricultural cycles are ingrained in Persephone's myth. Yet we can also view the timing of the Mysteries as a liminal time, on the edge of the light and dark halves of the year. Similarly, Persephone in her myth straddles the edge of the light (innocence and maidenhood) and dark (maturity and wisdom).

One of the key aspects of the Mysteries, was the consumption of a holy drink known as the "Kykeon". In Demeter's story, she asks Metaneira, the mother of the child she is caring for, to bring her a drink made of barley meal, water, and fresh pennyroyal (Shelmerdine, 1995). Architectural reliefs from Demeter's temple in Eleusis show the Kykeon vessel that held the sacred drink. This drink was given to initiates after their ritual fasting was complete and is believed to have contained a mixture of barley, leaves of a member of the mint family and possibly pennyroyal.

The most controversial ingredient believed by some historians to have been used is that of ergot, a fungus found in certain strains of wheat which is said to contain a psychotropic agent (Reif, 1999). Ergot can cause an ecstatic, hallucinogenic experience but it is also highly toxic. The drug known commonly as LSD can be derived from certain strains of ergot (https://www.britannica.com/science/LSD). A Czechoslovakian psychiatrist by the name of Stanislav Grof treated people with LSD in the 1960s and 1970s and found that a good number of these people re-experienced birth (Campbell, 1998). While we don't know exactly how the Kykeon and its inherent intoxicating effects impacted initiates it is likely based on what we do know about the impacts of ergot and LSD that the sacred drink played a pivotal role in the rites of the Greater Mysteries.

The Greater Mysteries officially began when the religious figure known as the "Hierokenyx" made an official proclamation of the opening of the festivities (Preka-Alexandri, 1997). Participants then purified themselves, usually through ritual bathing in the sea. Each initiate was expected to sacrifice a young pig and would then fast at home for a day. The choice of a pig for the sacrifice was deliberate. Pigs appear in many goddess myths, sometimes as a sacred animal and sometimes as an animal to be feared or overcome. Pigs have traditionally been associated with the moon, cycles of life and death and the Underworld. The sow played a significant role in the festival of Thesmophoria, seen as a precursor to the Eleusinian Mysteries as mentioned earlier. Women participating in the festival would at some point dig up the remains of pig sacrifices from an earlier festival and mix them with seeds to produce a good crop (https://www. britannica.com/topic/Thesmophoria).

The Greater Mysteries kicked off in earnest with the sacred procession, a journey to Eleusis from what is now known as the Kerameikos Cemetery in Athens. Initiates walked from Athens to Eleusis, stopping at times to offer sacrifices and perform sacred dances. At different points throughout the procession, altars and shrines were set up where participants would offer additional sacrifices and chant hymns. When the participants arrived at the bridge at the Kephisos River - the boundary between Athens and Eleusis-masked participants told raunchy jokes and made obscene gestures in a re-enactment of Iambe trying to cheer Demeter up in the "Hymn to Demeter" (Shelmerdine, 1995).

Priestesses in the procession carried boxes containing holy objects to be revealed during the formal rites. Because of the time it took to walk from Athens to Eleusis, torches must have been used to guide the way during the final stages of the procession. In addition to having a practical purpose, the use of torches would simulate Demeter wandering with a torch in search of her daughter. The procession ended at the outer court of the sanctuary in Eleusis where the priests of the cult welcomed the initiates.

Following the arrival of the participants, sacred dances would be performed by the Kalichoron Well near the front of the sanctuary (Stehle, 2007). This was followed by a day of rest. The following evening, the rites would begin. While we can't know the specifics of the rites, we do know that they involved a re-enactment of parts of Persephone's story, including her abduction into the Underworld.

Initiates were led by dim torchlight into the darkness of the Telesterion otherwise known as the "Hall of Mysteries". It was in the Telesterion that the formal ceremony took place and initiates experienced the "final revelation" (Stehle, 2007). According to information on placards at Eleusis, the Telesterion was a large hall with seats on all four sides where initiates sat and watched the rituals. The hierophants displayed sacred objects, recited sacred texts, and in some way conveyed to the participants a favorable view of life after death.

At some point, each initiate knelt, veiled. It is believed that each initiate held an unlit torch and a snake or representation of a snake while a fan of some sort was waved above their head (Uzzell, 2017). The snake is well known throughout the myths of many diverse cultures as being a symbol of regeneration; the snake sheds its old skin to be born again. Finally, a gong was struck and the Hierophant called upon Kore to emerge from the Underworld and be reunited with her mother. The priestess playing Persephone then emerged from the cave of Plouton which leads into the Underworld. This cave could easily have been seen from the site of the Telesterion as they were in close proximity.

It is believed that there may also have been an announcement that Persephone had given birth and, in silence a cut blade of wheat or an ear of corn was revealed. (Shelmerdine, 1995; Reif, 1999). While the meaning of these objects is a mystery, the wheat and corn can be interpreted as being a symbolic representation of the new life that Persephone has birthed. This is comparable to the sacred bread or wafer of wheat representing the body of Christ during Communion. However the rites were enacted, it would seem that participants in some way experienced being Kore and Demeter.

By experiencing being Kore and Demeter, the initiates also experienced the feeling of being planted in the barren ground in a seemingly lifeless state and then blossoming and emerging back into life, having been rebirthed. Having shared through the rites the suffering that Demeter and Persephone felt, it was believed by the initiates that they were rewarded by being assured of prosperity in their life and a favorable fate after death (Stehle, 2007).

The day following the ritual, initiates honored the dead with libations from special vases (Reif, 1999). According to Stehle in the book "Finding Persephone", on the final day:

"...two vessels of water were overturned to the East and the West as the throng cried out 'rain' to the sky and 'conceive' to the Earth." (Stehle, 1995, 176)

There were sacrifices of larger animals and feasting occurred before participants returned home. The Mysteries went on for many years until Christianity gradually spread and took hold. Finally, in 379 A. D. Theodosius I forbade the ancient cults and their practices (Preka-Alexandri, 1997). The sanctuary at Eleusis was finally destroyed in 395 A. D. as a result of the invasion of the Visigoths (Preka-Alexandri, 1997).

There is no way for us to know just what comprised the transcendental experience of the rites, but based on writings from ancient Greek philosophers and others who underwent the rites, it is safe to assume that the experience of initiation was powerful and life changing; providing participants with a sense of peace about death where once there was only fear. The duality of life and death plays a central role in the Mysteries, just as it does in Persephone's myth. The Neo-Platonic philosopher Proclus believed that initiation and physical death were closely linked. Proclus asserted that the transformation that the initiate underwent as part of the Greater Mysteries was very similar to the journey that the soul undergoes during death.

According to Proclus:

"At first, there are wanderings and laborious circuits and journeys through the dark, full of misgivings, where there is no consummation. Then, before the very end, come terrors of every kind, shivers and trembling and sweat and amazement. After this, a wonderful light meets the wanderer. He is admitted into pure meadows lands..." (Uzzell, 2017)

This is where Persephone's myth and the Great Mysteries can be of great assistance in our personal growth. Just as the seed must be planted in the cold, dark ground in order to eventually flourish, we, too, must be willing to descend into our darkness and experience a metaphorical death. This is the cost of enacting our personal power and attaining our sovereignty. Just as the soul must traverse the "laborious circuits" in the dark and just as the initiates of the Greater Mysteries must take a leap of faith into the unknown, we must be willing to stumble through our own shadowy realms in order to eventually experience the "wonderful light" that brings us closer to manifesting our full potential and finding great peace and happiness.

Journal Questions

- Have you ever participated in a "mystery" rite? If so, what was it like? How did you feel both before and after the ritual? What aspects of the ritual were the most powerful or impactful?
- Why do you think there was such a strong emphasis placed on secrecy? How did secrecy make the Mysteries

more effective?

- What are your views about physical death? What emotions does it evoke? Are you afraid of death and, if so, why?
- In what way has your religious upbringing (or lack thereof) influenced your views on death?
- A dark night of the soul can be described as a painful period of spiritual desolation and growth. Have you ever experienced a dark night of the soul? If so, how did you pull yourself out of it? What did you learn from the experience?
- Proclus compared initiation to a physical death. Think about any initiations you have undergone. These could be formal initiations such as initiation into a religious tradition or they could be more subtle initiations such as the breakup of your first serious relationship. In what ways did these initiations similar to the concept of death? What lessons or changes were provoked by these initiations?
- Why do you think the Eleusinian Mysteries had such a powerful impact on its participants?

Chapter 3

Descent and Ascent

As famous mythologists such as Joseph Campbell can attest, we can learn more about ourselves by exploring the archetypes and goddesses, particularly those that we feel the most strongly connected to. By delving into these goddesses and their myths, we can begin to see patterns that may reflect our own lives and thus can help us to predict future paths and pitfalls and hopefully save us from unnecessary pain and suffering (Bolen, 1984). This requires complete self-honesty and an in depth exploration of our own woundedness and the inner demons that haunt us. As Campbell states:

> *"One thing that comes out in myths, for example, is that at the bottom of the abyss comes the voice of salvation. The black moment is the moment when the real message of transformation is going to come. At the darkest moment comes the light."* (Campbell, 1988, 39)

Persephone's myth is one of descent and ascent; a journey that we all must take throughout our lives. In order to ascend into the light of our conscious potential and personal power, we must first descend into the shadowy realm of our own Underworld- the subconscious. If we undertake the journey with intention, we can experience unparalleled growth. However, if we refuse to embrace or even acknowledge this journey, we can often find ourselves stagnant and our lives-or some area(s) of our lives- may feel stuck. Descent can be terrifying, though for some ascent can be daunting as well. The journey requires a willingness to be vulnerable and an almost blind trust and leap of faith as we find ourselves enveloped in darkness.

The refusal to probe the wounds and fears buried in our subconscious doesn't eliminate the power that these wounds and fears have over us. Quite the opposite, for ignoring our shadow selves only intensifies their power. Refusing to acknowledge our accumulated pain and the things that scare us the most doesn't make them go away. They may lurk in the darkness of our subconscious but they will influence our actions, perspectives, and decisions often without our knowledge or awareness.

The analogy that I feel best describes this is that of a car. When we have done the inner work necessary to grow, we are in control of our vehicle and thus we are the only ones determining which turns to take and which paths to follow. The car of the person that is reacting from their subconscious is akin to that of a training car in a driver's education course wherein the instructor can take control of the vehicle at any time. Our subconscious takes control of our vehicle quite often without us ever realizing that there is someone else with the power to steer. The belief that we are in sole control of our vehicle is an illusion.

Fortunately, we find in Persephone an invaluable ally and guide. Persephone's myth is unusual in that it allows us to see ourselves in a deity that appears vulnerable and helpless. These feelings of vulnerability and helplessness are universally experienced at some point in our own lives, especially in our youth. The challenge comes when we are not able to move through these feelings and grow. It is necessary to have the courage to willingly face our own inner Underworld if we are to experience healing and growth.

Persephone's story can strongly resonate with those of us who have felt victimized at any point in our lives; particularly if we felt powerless and/or traumatized in our youth. As a child with a medical condition that rendered me to appear and feel weak and vulnerable, I resonated strongly with Persephone, particularly in her aspect as Kore. Here was someone - a goddess, no less - whose destiny was determined by those around her. Just as it did not appear to be present in my own life, the concept of personal power was nowhere to be found in Persephone's story. Persephone in her incarnation as Kore is the wounded, innocent girl who has difficulty saying no and asserting her own boundaries. As such, she becomes somewhat of a martyr.

I can identify many ways in which Persephone's Kore attributes manifested within me. I was a people pleaser, afraid to rock the boat for fear that someone would be upset with me. My fragile physical state made me feel as though I had nothing to offer the world other than to be acquiescent. Being nice became my currency and I was malleable, shifting to match the attributes and personality characteristics of those around me. Similarly, Persephone is a chameleon of sorts. She is the young maiden her mother wants her to be while with Demeter, but she transforms into the confident, powerful woman that Hades' desires when she is by his side.

Kore aligned individuals may find themselves being dishonest at times in order to avoid displeasing others or sharing unwelcome information. This is particularly true when we are children. As a result of our unwillingness to speak our truth, we often end up bottling up our own anger until it explodes. Like Persephone, we may feel that we cannot trust ourselves because the messages we receive from those around us lead us to believe that we are not capable of making our own decisions.

Those who resonate with Persephone in both her Kore and Queen forms have a tendency to be preoccupied with the inner world. I spent hours in my room for much of my childhood simply reading, daydreaming, imagining, and thinking. Yet, there is a unique gift to be found within our Persephone aspect, and that is the gift of receptivity. Ironically, the compulsion to please others and the ability to know what others want or need can manifest as a high sensitivity and empathic ability. These gifts can be invaluable tools to help us journey within; yet, if we do not push ourselves through descent and into ascent we may find ourselves experiencing depression (Bolen, 1984).

There is another dilemma that arises as a result of an unwillingness to move from Kore to Queen. The child that perpetuates people pleasing tendencies may eventually find that their entire life's purpose revolves around making others happy. This may work if we have spouses and/or children to please but at some point as children move out of the house or a marriage ends, we find that we need to start living our lives for ourselves. The individual whose life revolved around others must now stand alone and they may not have any clue as to who they are or what they want after years of being rewarded for making others happy (Bolen, 1984).

Dr. Jean Shinoda Bolen in her groundbreaking book entitled "Goddesses in Every Woman" states that the vulnerable goddesses - and thus those that identify strongly with them - typically go through three phases. The first phase is a happy, innocent phase wherein the goddess feels protected and wants for nothing. She typically does not have any exposure to a life that is less than idyllic. In the second phase, the goddess becomes the victim of someone or something, and she has little to no ability to influence her own fate. The final phase is achieved only if the goddess or individual is willing and able to garner the courage to complete what Joseph Campbell refers to as the "hero's journey". This necessitates facing the reality of the situation and acknowledging an ability to act and speak for one's self. This final phase is a period of restoration or transformation (Bolen, 1984).

One can pass quickly through any or all of these phases, or we may find ourselves remaining for an extended period of time in one particular phase. In addition, we may find ourselves repeating these phases again and again throughout our lives, peeling away layers each time in order to get closer and closer to our own purest essence and truth. Persephone reminds us that while we can't control others or external factors which may place us in a position of being victimized, we can choose how we react to these situations and whether or not we allow them to ultimately strengthen us or weaken us. The ability to act from a place of consciousness rather than involuntarily reacting from our shadow selves is the core gift of sovereignty.

Facing the darkness is not an easy task and can be quite painful and frightening. As Queen, Persephone reigned over several Underworld rivers including Acheron, the River of Pain. Despite being a lesser known Underworld river-particularly as compared to the river Styx-Acheron was one of the most important rivers of the Underworld. It was believed that souls had to cross over Acheron as they journeyed to the afterlife (Brannen, 2018).

In much the same way, we must explore our wounds and face our pain if we are to cross over into reclaiming our power. If we do not confront our pain, our pain will have power over us. In order to achieve clarity, we must first look deeply into ourselves - both the light and dark aspects. Growth always requires a sacrifice or a letting go of something. While the shadows created by the wound sustained in our early years are often painful, they are typically born out of a sincere desire to protect ourselves and thus serve some function early on. Sometimes the choices we have made in the past that foster the growth of our wounds were the best choices that we knew how to make in that particular moment in our lives. Unfortunately, these same survival and coping mechanisms typically don't serve us well as we move into adulthood.

When we bear Kore's wounds and align ourselves with her (without conscious knowledge of doing so), we may find ourselves repeatedly attracted to situations and/or people that diminish our sense of personal power (www.goddesspower. com). This feeling of powerlessness can crop up at any time in our adult lives if we have not intentionally and thoroughly sought to heal our wounds and let go of outdated beliefs about ourselves and our abilities. As I grew older and fought to gain my independence and control over my own life, I began to see Persephone's story in a new and inspirational light. Although it may appear that Persephone exerts no control at any point in her myth, if we dig deeper we can see that her story is actually one of moving from a young, seemingly helpless child to that of a confident, self-determined woman.

Growing beyond our wounds and grasping our own power means that we can no longer surrender responsibility for our lives and instead must make conscious choices and be accountable for the implications of our actions. This is an abdication of our innocence and it is this innocence that Persephone had to sacrifice in order to become Hades' queen. When you meet your darkness, you lose your innocence but you gain wisdom and personal power. By listening to the message our wounds have to share, we can achieve greater clarity and gently remove the shackles that our wounds have placed upon us. Looking for the sacred message inherent in our pain can result in powerful healing that is transformative.

Fortunately, we have a psychopomp in the form of Persephone, who can offer comfort and guide us through our darkness as we work to find our way back into the light. As the Queen of the Underworld and as a guide for the deceased, Persephone can act as a guide by channeling her ability to "... move back and forth between the ego-based reality of the 'real' world or the archetypal reality of the psyche" (Bolen, 1984, 203). If we undertake the journey of descent with intention, a sort of alchemy occurs that makes us more powerful than before.

Persephone's myth reflects the work of descent and ascent in both the agricultural cycles inherent in the story and the symbolic cycles of birth, death and rebirth. The entire myth is a delicate dance between helplessness and power and loss and gain (Tzanetou, 2007). We can align our descent work with a seasonal cycle; however, it is important to note that the Mediterranean growing season didn't follow agricultural cycles in America and other parts of Europe.

Throughout both Persephone's myth and the Eleusinian Mysteries, agricultural symbolism was used metaphorically to denote spiritual growth. In Greece, grain was planted in the fall and germinated for a few weeks before growing throughout the winter (Shelmerdine, 1995). The grain ripened and was harvested in the spring and early summer (Reif, 1999). The grains that were harvested in the summer were placed in silos to be preserved in ground. Thus, the grains which were the wealth of the community were considered to be in the keep of the underworld (Campbell, 1990). At some point, Hades began to be referred to as the god Pluto, who was often shown with an overflowing cornucopia.

The pomegranate, symbol of the goddess Persephone, flowered in the early summer and ripened in the fall after the threshed grain had been stored in silos (Reif, 1999). The fact that the pomegranate, a symbol of fertility, ripens at a time when most of the land is dormant offers the lesson that even in our times of darkness growth may still occur. Thus while we typically think of winter and darkness as being barren and impotent, the pomegranate and the grain stored in silos were indicative of a belief by the ancient Greeks that there was treasure to be found in the Underworld and the dark.

There is another lesson to be found in the correlation between Persephone's myth and agricultural cycles. The cycle of growth for wheat is in a sense eternal as the seed is planted, the plant is cut and dies and yet is the source of its own regeneration (Reif, 1999). Similarly, Persephone is born, grows to be a maiden and then her maidenhood and innocence dies. She descends into the Underworld and through her union with Hades and with death itself she is reborn into a confident woman. She is the source of her own regeneration. Instead of fighting against her circumstances and environment, she uses both to foster her renewal and restoration, albeit in a different form. Her ability to reconcile her incarnation as Kore with her incarnation as a goddess and Queen of the Underworld leads to greater self-awareness (Reif, 1999).

When we meet our darkness for the first time, we lose our innocence and things can never go back to the way they were. Yet the great reward is that we gain the wisdom and confidence necessary to manifest our personal power and experience greater freedom and fulfillment. Death is a process of letting go and is a necessary part of transformation. Often when we do inner work, we find that we must let something of value die-whether it is a relationship, a belief, an aspect of ourselves, a job, and/or a way of living. The act of letting go is hard and can be unbearably painful; yet it is necessary for something new and better to be born.

It is not enough though to simply let go, however, as we must consciously grieve that which we know we may no longer hold onto. This, too, is part of the work of descent. It is in this seemingly fallow period that we may mourn, rest and recuperate. Allowing ourselves to hibernate for a time in the darkness gives us the opportunity to heal, reflect, and integrate the lessons we have learned. After a time, what once felt like a tomb now begins to feel like a womb and we start to awake to the possibilities that a new beginning can bring as we prepare to emerge into the light. Experiencing the process of descent and ascent results in the realization that we can be both vulnerable and strong at the same time.

It is upon our emergence from descent that we reap the rewards of the work we have undertaken. Once Persephone has completed her journey from naive girl to sovereign queen, she represents the potential for new growth, the ability to be flexible and have an open mind, the gift of strong intuition, and the capacity to direct her destiny and claim what she wants for herself. She becomes comfortable in her own skin and has learned to trust and love herself. Embracing her roles as both maiden of Spring and Queen of the Underworld, Persephone embodies sovereignty.

The Work of Descent
Guided Meditation: Laying Your Labels to Rest

One of the first steps in the intentional descent into our own Underworld is to learn to see ourselves more clearly. In order to better understand who we are, we must first recognize who and what we are not. Symbolically separating the grain that comprises our essence from the chaff of illusions initiates the process of letting go.

Often times, we find ourselves taking on roles or labels that others give to us without ever really considering whether or not they are accurate or align with what it is we truly want. We also impose judgemental labels on ourselves based on our own inner self critic and who we think we should be. We may feel comfortable or compelled to play the role of the selfless mother whose family always comes first, the employee who devotes all of her time to her work, or the peacemaker who is hesitant to rock the boat. Perhaps we weren't good at something as a child or we were felt that we were clumsy and these perceptions continue to color how we see ourselves even after many years have gone by.

When we take the time to analyze whether or not these labels and roles ring true, it is not uncommon for us to find that we are not acting in alignment with our authentic selves and our innermost desires. Even good labels can be troublesome. You might be good at math and be encouraged to go into accounting by those around you (with the best of intentions) when really, deep down, you want to be an artist. The guided meditation that follows will help you to identify what labels you have been carrying around and release those which inhibit rather than act as a catalyst for your personal power and happiness.

Sit in a comfortable position and close your eyes. Pay close attention to your breathing. Breathe in and out slowly for a few cycles until you are ready to begin. In your mind's eye, you see a door in front of you. This could be any type of door...a large wooden door, a glass door, even a portal. When you are ready, step through the door.

You notice that it is twilight, and the land around you seems cold and barren. You pull your dark cloak around you as you shiver. Ahead, you see what appears to be the mouth of a cave and a beautiful young woman standing a few feet away. You make your way towards the cave and the woman greets you. Despite her beauty and her youthful appearance, her voice conveys maturity, self-assuredness, and strength. She takes your hand and begins to tell you more about the cave.

"I am Persephone, Queen of the Underworld. This cave is the entrance to the Underworld, the place where souls must begin their journey to the afterlife. Although you are still very much alive, you will be undertaking a similar journey of death and rebirth. By descending into the darkness below, you will release those aspects of yourself which no longer align with your truth and which serve only to burden you as you strive for happiness and fulfillment of your potential. Throughout our lives, we allow others to define us. We may strive to nurture and please others in order to fulfill their vision of us. If we do so without consciously considering whether or not these definitions are truly accurate, we end up sacrificing ourselves. We become stagnant, frozen forever poised on the precipice of our own potential and power.

Inside the cave, you will see that there is a staircase leading down deep into the bowels of the Earth. This staircase is lit only by torches but I assure you that you will be able to find your way despite the dim light. As you make your way down this staircase, I ask that you travel deep within yourself as well. I ask that you identify the many parts which you feel compelled to play; the labels you wear which are imposed upon you by others, society, even yourself. Dwell within each of them, explore them, feel the weight of them, just as you have inhabited their energy in your day to day life. I implore you to think about how these labels have held you back from realizing your personal power and, perhaps, how they have dishonored and shamed you or caused you pain.

Should you choose to undertake this journey, I assure you I will be waiting for you once you complete your descent. Although I will not be there in person to guide you, I will be there beside you in spirit."

Persephone pauses, and then asks you if you are ready to undertake this journey. You are not sure if you are strong enough to do this, but you know you have to try. You brace yourself for what lies ahead and nod to indicate that you are ready. Persephone leads you to the top of the stairway. You can see that the stairs spiral down, at times weaving in and out of what appear to be open rooms or tunnels. You realize that you cannot see where the staircase ends.

Calling upon all of your courage, you take a deep breath and place your foot on the first step. As you descend the stairs, you begin thinking of the labels that you have worn throughout your life, as well as the labels that you are still carrying around. You start with the simple labels and expectations others have used to define who you are and/or who you should be as a mother, woman, employee, a partner, a friend. As you name each label and consider its meanings and implications, you feel increasing pressure as though your cloak has been weighted down. While you cannot see them, you sense ghost like creatures hovering behind you. You instinctively know that these ghosts are the shades present in Underworld legends. From time to time, they whisper in your ear, trying to convince you that the labels are accurate.

You continue your introspection and find that identifying the labels and what they mean to you is becoming more difficult and intimidating. With the naming of each label or expectation, the pressure on your cloak feels more and more daunting and the whispers of the shades become louder and louder. The light becomes dimmer, yet you manage to continue to make your way down the steps. Just when you think you can't move one more step, you see Persephone's face and realize that you have reached the bottom of the staircase. Persephone smiles and embraces you. The air smells dank, and you hear the gentle lapping of water.

You follow Persephone over to a river. You look down and are startled by your own reflection. You don't recognize the woman staring back at you, as she is hunched over and burdened by an enormous dark, shadowy cloaks that coil around her. The cloak threatens to suffocate you and feel paralyzed. You realize that the heavy energy you have been carrying around is a culmination of every label or belief you have allowed to be placed upon. These labels have worn you down in ways you hadn't before realized, chaining you to the shadows that lurk within, and stunting your ability to see clearly.

You look up and notice a dark figure in a boat coming towards you. Persephone tells you that in order for rebirth to occur, there must be a death; a letting go. She tells you that in order to cross back into the light, you must offer payment to the guide navigating the ferry. You protest that you have nothing to give. Persephone looks deep into your eyes and places her hands on your cloak. You realize that in order to claim your power and gain your freedom, you must let go of that which has burdened you. Your ardent desire to remove your cloak causes the shades that have been circling around you to shriek in protest.

Despite their cries and despite the weight that you have been carrying, you manage to remove the cloak and you hand it to the man in the boat.

"Well done, my child", Persephone says as she embraces you once more. Your journey took great courage and you will find that though others may feel challenged by your decision to shed those labels that do not align with who you know yourself to be, *the reward will ultimately be as great as the journey has been daunting. Persephone assures you that she will be here for you, waiting, should you ever need her guidance or feel the need to once again shed your "skin" and be resurrected in authenticity.*

You thank Persephone and step into the boat. The boat seems to move forward of its own accord and while it seems to move slowly, you reach the other side as if no time has passed. The guide silently steps out of the boat and motions for you to follow him. He makes his way to a room with a blazing fire. As though it is a funeral pyre, he lays the cloak to rest in the flames and you feel conflicting emotions as you watch the labels carried by the cloak that once seemed such an integral part of you turn to smoke and ash. When the fire has subsided and there is no more evidence of the cloak, the guide points towards an uphill path leading out of the cave and you understand that you are to make your way up the path.

With each step upwards, you feel lighter and lighter, as though you were weightless. Joy surges through you and you feel a freedom unlike anything you have felt since you were a child. When you finally reach the top of the hill, you walk into a clearing in the full light of day. Flowers are blooming and the trees are alive with lush, green foliage. You see a stream in the distance and you run towards it. As you bend down to take a drink, you see yourself. You are beautiful and glowing, as if lit from within. Once you have had a chance to refresh yourself, you stand and make your way towards a door that appears in the distance. It is the same door that you encountered at the beginning of this meditation. When you are ready, you walk back through the door. Take a few moments to return your attention to your breathing and when you are feeling grounded, open your eyes.

Journal Questions-Descent

- Write about your experiences with the meditation. How did the meditation make you feel? Were there any labels that came up that surprised you?

- What labels did you have the hardest time letting go of during the meditation? What labels felt as though they may have had a seed of truth in them?
- Which labels do you feel were imposed upon you by others? Can you recall how that happened and/or when the label took hold?
- Which labels were imposed upon you by yourself? What do you think caused this to occur?
- Were there any positive labels that you released because they did not feel to align with your core essence? If so, what were they?
- In the meditation, the "shades" follow you throughout your journey and they scream at you when they realize that you are disposing of the labels that they have helped to reinforce. Do you have inner voices that act as shades? Do you have people in your life that - knowingly or not - speak to you in ways that reinforce the negative beliefs or labels that you carry around? If so, how can you begin to lessen the power of these voices (both your own and others)?
- What scares you the most about delving into your own shadows? What might you be able to do to help alleviate or work through this fear?
- Think for a moment about past wounds, beliefs and/or fears that you carry with you. Are there specific ones that you feel are having an impact on your life in some way now? Which of the wounds, beliefs, and/or fears do you feel are most daunting and/or powerful?
- What purpose have your wounds, beliefs and fears served? How might they have helped you in some way at one point?

Journal Questions-Ascent

- Now that you have worked to rid yourself of labels and

beliefs that no longer serve you, how do you wish to fill the void? What beliefs and/or roles do you wish to embrace?

- How will your life look and feel different if you are, like Persephone, able and willing to let go of old beliefs and embrace personal and spiritual growth?

- Think about who in your life can support you through this process of transformation. How can they provide support? Are there other groups or individuals that are not currently in your life that might be able to help? Identify a support network that you might be able to rely on as challenges arise.

- We know that Persephone can act as a guide through the dark Underworld of our souls. How do you think she might be able to help you once you have ascended back into the light? In what ways can you work with her to solicit her wisdom, guidance and support?

- While descent can be quite daunting, surprisingly ascent can be intimidating as well as we are no longer able to hide in the darkness and instead either fail or succeed under the bright light of emergence. Having faced our fears, we must now act. How will you move your vision forward? What small steps can you begin to take to embrace and enact your personal power?

Chapter 4

Persephone as Psychopomp

Persephone's roles as both Queen of the realm of the dead and life giving Goddess of Spring may seem contradictory at first glance. Yet, there are many examples of goddesses throughout history who held the power of both life and death in their hands. Within these goddesses were all forces - active and passive, and creative and destructive (Spretnak, 1992). Death and birth were seen as part of a natural whole, and the goddess oversaw the cycle itself. Similarly, each of us also has the capacity to create and destroy.

According to Charlene Spretnak, in Paleolithic times the Goddess was worshipped as the embodiment of Earth (1992). With this perspective in mind, caves were seen as both wombs and tombs. Rituals took place within the darkness of the earth's womb, at times with the intent of manifesting what the people of the land wanted or needed. The dead were also returned to the cave for burial and passage to the afterlife. It is therefore not surprising that the entrance to the Underworld in Persephone's myth is a cave.

Both Persephone and her mother Demeter were seen as chthonic deities connected to agriculture. In Athens, the dead were called "Demetreioi, 'Demeter's People'" (Spretnak, 1992, 106). Hecate as well is often believed to have associations with the dead. In some ways, Persephone encapsulates the archetypes of maiden, mother and crone. Early on in her story, she is portrayed as being a young and innocent maiden. Her mothering aspect manifests in the way that she is said to nurture and comfort the dead when in the Underworld. By the end of the story, she oversees the realm of the dead and has acquired wisdom and clarity that only comes with life experience. In Parmenides' philosophical poem about a poet's journey to the afterlife, Persephone is described as being a benevolent goddess, there to teach the poet truth (Serena Mirto, 2012).

Persephone demonstrates mothering, nurturing qualities as she brings comfort to the dead. In Charlene Spretnak's retelling of Persephone's myth, she chooses to go to the Underworld upon glimpsing the souls of the dead in pain as they are lost and confused with no one to guide or comfort them (Spretnak, 1992). Persephone acts as a guide for the dead; showing them the more beautiful aspects of the Underworld and helping them to see "...the knowledge of their own divinity" (Reif, 1999, 55). Persephone is not only ruler of the Underworld (with Hades by her side), she is also the navigator for its inhabitants. Thus, she may also aide us as a psychopomp.

A psychopomp is a guide within the realm of souls. A psychopomp can work directly with souls by leading them to and/or guiding them within the realm of the dead. A psychopomp can also work with the living who are trying to access those who have passed over. In this function, the psychopomp's role is to protect the well-being of the seeker, to ensure that the seeker does not get lost and arrives to their destination safely, and to help the seeker access the information being sought (Farrar, Bone, 2016). In addition to acting as a guide through the Underworld, the psychopomp can also help us to access other shadowy realms, such as the realm of the unconscious and/or the spiritual realm of the gods. As one example, psychopomps were used at the Oracle of Delphi to assist the Pythia (Farrar, Bone, 2016).

Accessing Ancestral Wisdom

Various artifacts of ancient Greece illustrate the central role women played in dialoguing with the dead via acts such as lamentation and tomb side rituals (Serena Mirto, 2012). Through these actions, the wife or mother of the deceased would address their loved one as though he or she were able to hear them (Serena Mirto, 2012). Though views of what happened in the afterlife changed and evolved over time, artifacts from the later periods of ancient Greece point to a belief that the deceased retained some of their memories and feelings and could appreciate funeral rites and offerings made on their behalf, such as perfume, oil, and honey. Gold leaf tablets found in Thessaly, Macedonia, Crete and Southern Italy were inscribed with instructions for the deceased including "passwords" to be given when arriving in Hades so that the Gods would know that the deceased had been initiated into the Mysteries and purified and so that they could drink from the Spring of Mnemosyne (memory) should they so desire (Serena Mirto, 2012).

There were various descriptions given of Hades by poets and philosophers over time. These descriptions included but were not limited to a realm hidden in a misty fog at the edge of the Earth containing beaches and sacred woods of poplars and willows, a walled city with large entrance gates and a dreamlike atmosphere, and a dark, cave like environment with rivers (Serena Mirto, 2012). It was not uncommon for individuals to try and find a way to communicate with their deceased loved ones and in 5th century Athens the cult of the dead existed as a way to accomplish this goal (Serena Mirto, 2012). Perhaps the most well-known location for attempting to communicate with deceased loved ones was the Nekromanteion at Ephyra, Greece.

The Nekromanteion can be found on the river Acheron in Epirus. The individual seeking to make contact with the deceased would be purified by priests before entering from the East and making offerings to ancestors and gods in a pit (Farrar, Bone 2016). The seeker would then walk through a labyrinthine maze while a priest invoked the spirits of the dead as well as the goddesses Hecate and Persephone (Farrar Bone, 2016). The tunnels and maze were intended to create the illusion that the seeker was walking through the streets of Hades. Finally, the seeker would come to a central hall where an offering of barley would be placed on the floor of the chamber for Hades and

Persephone and the seeker would enter a dark chamber or cave to communicate with the spirits (Farrar Bone, 2016).

This was not a simple or brief undertaking. The chambers of the Nekromanteion were said to be very dark and could take hours or even days to traverse. This, along with the priests' recitation of magical incantations and the anticipation of speaking with the deceased must have impacted the mindset of the seeker so that he or she ultimately felt as if they were moving through the realm of the dead themselves. Yet, despite the immersion of the seeker into this Underworld like atmosphere, there is still some question as to just how far into the realm of the dead the seeker metaphorically traveled as some believed that it was not safe for one to come in to full contact with the dead.

The Realm of the Ancestors is considered by many to be the "collective unconscious" (Farrar Bone). Our ancestors can help us to find answers that seem to be outside of our grasp. In many cases, our ancestors support and help us unseen. While we tend to think of ancestors as blood relatives from our past, ancestors can include those individuals related to us by marriage or adoption as well as those who came before us in a particular field that we are passionate about, be it healing, a particular spiritual practice, or a vocation.

For the purposes of the guided meditation that is to follow, I recommend starting with attempting to contact an ancestor that is a relative with whom you either had a positive relationship in this life or one that perhaps you have never met but know about, are familiar with and feel a resonance with. I would advise that you not try to seek out an ancestor with whom you may have had past issues with and/or who may have threatened the well-being of others while alive. It is helpful, though not necessary, to have a picture of or an item belonging to the ancestor you are trying to contact near you. Alternately, you could have an item to represent something that you know this ancestor was fond of or connected to while they were alive.

The use of sound - such as through lamentation, chanting, or invocations - was an important part of ancient Greek funerary rites and attempts to contact the spirit world. As mentioned above, magical incantations were an integral piece of the Nekromanteion experience. There is an invocation included in the guided meditation; however, feel free to replace it with a chant or your own heartfelt words should you so desire. Listening to shamanic drumming at 220-240 beats per minute is very helpful for inducing trance states to help you move deeper into the meditation. You can typically find this type of drumming via Youtube and on some smart phone apps.

Guided Meditation - Visiting the Ancestors

Sit in a comfortable position and close your eyes. Pay close attention to your breathing. Breathe in and out slowly for a few cycles until you are ready to begin. In your mind's eye, you see a door in front of you. This could be any type of door...a large wooden door, a glass door, even a portal. When you are ready, step through the door.

You find yourself on a hill at twilight. You can see below you what appears to be a cave. The air is a little chilly, and you pull your cloak more closely around you. You follow a path to your left down the hill and approach the entrance of the first tunnel. Persephone is waiting for you. She asks if you wish to visit the realm of your ancestors and you state that you do. She explains that to do so you must make your way into the cave and through the maze of tunnels which will take you to the portion of the Underworld that houses your ancestors. There will be some stops along the way, she says, but you will know what to do when the time comes. Persephone smiles, hands you a torch, and says that she will see you on the other size of the maze. You look at the dark tunnel before you. Its walls are lined with torches yet the further you look down the tunnel's path, the more it seems like an endless black void. With some trepidation, you enter the tunnel and begin walking.

The airs smells dank, as if there is a water source somewhere.

Your hands glide along the smooth, cold walls. The sound is a heavy stillness, similar to the sound you hear when you are underwater. The path curves and twists, sometimes leading to a crossroads where you must choose, other times winding in circles that seem to lead you back. Each time you are faced with a crossroads, you instinctively take the path to the left. Time seems to lose all meaning and you feel yourself soothed in a trance by the simple act of making your way through the tunnels. The paths wind and turn for what seems like hours until finally you arrive at a clearing.

In front of you is an altar stone, with offering bowls on either side. Persephone steps forward out of the darkness of what appears to be the entrance to another tunnel or cave. You reach into your cloak and take out a handful of barley and a libation of some sort. You put each of these into the offering bowls beside the altar. Persephone asks you to place on the altar a representation of the ancestor you wish to contact. You do so. She then asks your purpose in entering the ancestral realm, and you recite the following words:

I seek the wisdom of those who have gone before me
Loved in life, remembered in death
Whose blessings have brought me comfort
Whose strength has fed my resilience
Whose actions have blazed trails and paths that I may follow
And whose gifts I feel honored to share
Hear me, as I come to you with humility and respect
Seeking your knowledge, your wisdom
Feel me, feel my love and gratitude for you
See me, one of your line, one of your heart
Show me, tell me the answers that I seek
Please accept my offerings in your honor and in your name
Blessed be

When you are done, Persephone nods at you, and leads you into the next entrance and you follow her down a winding staircase.

Although it is hazy and the light is somewhat dim, you are overcome by a sense of serenity. There are rivers flowing on either side of you as Persephone leads you to an iron gate. Persephone opens the gate with ease and you see in front of you a raised chair facing what appears to be an island of some sort. The island is surrounded by rivers on either side and there is a stream connecting the two rivers, acting as a sort of moat in front of the island. Persephone instructs you to sit in the chair and explains that you will have the ability to speak with your ancestor should they be willing to speak with you, but that there is an unseen barrier dividing the island from where you are and that while Persephone as queen of the Underworld may cross the stream, neither you nor any of the inhabitants of the Underworld may do so.

Persephone asks you which of your ancestors you seek. You name the ancestor in question. As she approaches the stream, a bridge appears and she is greeted on the other side by what appears to be an older woman, dressed in a long black cloak with keys at her waist. The woman's face is hidden by her hood. Persephone whispers in her ear, and the woman walks away from her, with the intent of bringing your ancestor to you. You think carefully about what it is that you would ask of your ancestor as you know your time here is limited and your questions must be worded skillfully with intent for the greatest chance of clarity.

You sit on the raised seat, meditating upon your question until the hooded woman returns with the ancestor you have requested to speak with. Persephone returns to your side, and the bridge across the stream disappears with each step she takes. You greet your ancestor by name. If it is an ancestor that you have not previously met in this lifetime, you introduce yourself and explain how you are connected. With great honor and respect, you ask your ancestor for the information you have come to try to obtain.

Sit quietly and listen. It may take a few moments for you to receive a response. The answer you receive may come as though he or she is speaking to you, or it could be a vision or a knowing. The answer may not make sense at first, or you may receive general wisdom as opposed to a specific answer. You may ask clarifying questions, but be sure to do so sparingly. Try to take in any information that is being shared with you without judgement or expectation. It is not uncommon for information offered by the ancestral realm to not make sense at first but often the meaning unveils itself over the course of the next several days or weeks.

Take some time to simply absorb anything that is being shared by your ancestor. When you feel the time is right or when your ancestor indicates in some way that he or she is done, thank your ancestor and provide an offering. This could a general offering of food or libations or it could be something specific that you know your ancestor enjoyed during their lifetime. You then turn to Persephone and she reaches out her hand to guide you back into your current time and space. You walk back up the winding pathway, only this time when you emerge from the entrance you find that the tunnels are gone. It is dawn, and you can see the hill that was your starting point a little ways away. You make your way back up the hill and through the door that brought you to this place. When you are ready, you walk back through the door. Take a few moments to return your attention to your breathing and when you are feeling grounded, open your eyes. If you find that you need more grounding and/or do not feel like you have fully returned, place your hands on the ground for a bit and/or eat a snack. When you have fully grounded, take some time to record in your journal what was shared with you and what you experienced.

Accessing the Wisdom of Your Subconscious

Just as Persephone in her role of Queen of the Underworld can help us by acting as a psychopomp, she can also guide us through the metaphorical Underworld known as our subconscious. The metaphorical underworld is home to the symbols associated with archetypes and the collective unconscious as well as being home to our own shadows and demons. As Jean Shinoda Bolen points out,

"Symbolically, the underworld can represent deeper layers of the psyche, a place where memories and feelings have been buried." (1984, 202). It is in our subconscious that we hide away our fears and past traumas that we feel we cannot deal with.

The subconscious also holds space for the aspects of ourselves that we don't like or approve of and/or are ashamed of. Our personal underworld begins receiving these "guests" from early childhood, typically without our realizing it. While these thoughts, fears, and attributes reside in the dark that does not mean that they don't hold sway over our lives. In fact, quite the contrary is true.

The shadows of our subconscious are constantly influencing the way that we act and the choices that we make. A common example of this is when we find ourselves repeating patterns or ending up in undesirable situations and we have no idea why these things keep happening to us. Think of your body and mind as a car. You-your conscious self, have your hands on the steering wheel at all times and believe that you are in control of your vehicle. The subconscious is an invisible passenger with a steering wheel that can override the one you are using without your knowledge. If we are to enact our personal power, it is imperative that we explore our subconscious and face what we find there so that we can ultimately be in full conscious control of our actions or at the very least be aware of the impetus behind the choices we make that do not serve us.

Interestingly, we do access this shadowy realm on a regular basis often without realizing it. Our subconscious is active while we sleep, making itself known- albeit usually in indecipherable ways- in our sleep. Sleep is in many ways the living state most closely resembling death, and in this letting go of our conscious control, our subconscious has more freedom to make itself known (Serena Mirto, 2012). Yet, during our waking hours, our personal Underworld can seem like a dark and terrifying place. There is a reason we have chosen to exile feelings and memories to the darkness and there may be traumas from our past that we don't want to risk re-experiencing. Making the journey through our own Underworld can be fill us with paralyzing fear and can be both confusing and exhausting - so why make the journey at all?

Joseph Campbell provided us with perhaps the most compelling reason for undertaking this journey, for as he says, "The cave you fear to enter holds the treasure you seek". By facing our shadows we can eventually let go of painful beliefs that hold us back and ultimately reach the core of who we are and what we desire. Freedom and the ability to manifest the life that we want are the rewards to be found at the end of what may seem like a perilous quest. The work that we undertake in confronting our personal demons may also unleash a wellspring of creativity that we did not know we possessed.

If we look at aspects of Persephone's myth, we can see the treasures that our personal Underworld has to offer. As illustrated earlier, Persephone's journey through the Underworld results in her ability to embrace and manifest her sovereignty and make choices for herself rather than being a victim. Furthermore, in the classical period, Hades began to be known as a name for the Underworld rather than the god himself. The god known as Hades began to be referred to as Pluto, a title connected with the word "ploutos" which means wealth (Serena Mirto, 2012). According to author Serena Mirto, this change in title is "... reflective of his more benevolent role as guardian of the riches hidden in the bosom of the earth..." (2012, 22).

Just as there are riches hidden in the literal Underworld, so too are our treasures and greatest gifts also held deep in our subconscious. We must dig deep to the very bottom if we are to uncover all of them. Each time we dig, each time we make this journey, we find new and unexpected riches waiting to be uncovered. Persephone can help provide a light and guide our way as we journey into the dark. One way to work with her in this aspect, is to repeat the guided meditation entitled "Visiting the Ancestors", only this time when you announce your intent, ask to meet a shadow that is ready and willing to meet you and that will have the answers that would most likely benefit you in your life at this time.

When you see your shadow across the water, ask how he or she came to be and what their purpose is. Listen closely as they tell you their story. You might notice that while they may appear terrifying at first, their appearance may begin to shift and you might find yourself staring at a younger version of yourself by the time they are done talking. If that is the case and/or you feel compelled to comfort this shadow, you can simply ask Persephone to create a bridge so that your shadow may come to you.

As an alternate option and/or in addition to using the guided meditation in this way, you may also ask Persephone to have your shadow come visit you in your dreams. Specify that you wish this dream take place in an environment conducive to having an experience that is beneficial and which feels like a safe space. This may take several attempts so don't be discouraged if it doesn't happen on your first try. When you awake, before getting up try to remember and record anything that you recall about your dreams, even if it seems hazy or doesn't make sense.

Whichever method(s) you choose, be sure to thank Persephone and leave her offerings. You may want to consider leaving an offering to the shadow selves you encounter as well, for it is much more effective to develop a relationship with them (with you in the driver's seat) and learn from them then to alienate them and possibly inadvertently push them back into your subconscious.

Journal Questions - Ancestral Wisdom

- Think about the ancestor you chose to meet with in the guided meditation. Why did you choose this ancestor?

What wisdom did they share with you?

- How did it feel to walk through the tunnels to the Underworld? If you felt afraid or anxious, you may want to take some time to reflect on the underlying cause of this emotion and journal about it.
- Often times, ancestral or "mother" wounds can impact us in our lives without our awareness. Can you think of any ancestral wounds that might exist? If so, how do you think the energy and influence of these wounds might be playing out in your life?
- In what areas do you think accessing ancestral wisdom might help you to practice the art of personal power?

Journal Questions - Wisdom of Your Subconscious

- Think back on some of the powerful and/or transformative times in your life. What patterns appear to exist? How might your subconscious have played a role in these situations?
- Think of times in your past or your present where you made choices from a place of pain and/or with the influence of your shadow. What did you learn from this? What do you think created this particular shadow to being with?
- Take a look at your journal answers from Chapter 3, Descent. What additional insights do you now have regarding what purpose(s) your shadows may have served and how you might heal the wounds feeding these shadows?
- If you did the guided meditation replacing an ancestor with a shadow, write about your experiences in your journal. How did the shadow appear in the beginning of your interaction? Did your shadow change at all? If so, how?

Chapter 5

Persephone and the Art of Discernment

The art of discernment is a crucial ingredient in one's ability to wield personal power. Discernment is defined as the ability to judge well, the ability to perceive differences, and/or acute judgement and understanding. The skill of discernment allows us to penetrate the illusions that other people create about us and our lives as well as the illusions we create ourselves. Practicing discernment enables us to see things as they are, not as we want them to be and ultimately helps us to take personal responsibility for our own choices and actions. Discernment facilitates clear sight and in doing so sometimes helps us to see options and opportunities that we might not otherwise have noticed.

Being able to see clearly is just as important in our modern society as it was in ancient Greece. During the time Persephone's myth was written, women were not allowed a great deal of power or authority-not just over others but over their own lives as well. This is reflected in Homer's version of Persephone's myth as everyone around her feels is necessary and appropriate to make choices for Persephone without consideration for her input or desires. While it is true that women in today's society by and large have far more freedom and autonomy as compared to the women of ancient Greece, there are still those who would take away choices from women about their own rights and bodies if given the opportunity.

Not only is the autonomy of modern women challenged by some in the larger and more noticeable political arena, the way women are viewed in our society often results in many women experiencing challenges to their autonomy in far more insidious ways on a regular basis. Women who are highly sensitive in particular may find their empathic abilities working against them rather than for them as they make decisions about their own lives with the feelings and/or perceptions of those around them taking the highest priority. By working with Persephone and embracing the lessons inherent in her myth, we can learn to develop discernment and achieve greater clarity. In addition to possessing strong intuition, Persephone represents the potential for receptivity, flexibility, growth and an open mind (Bolen, 1984).

We often don't realize that we lack discernment in our decision making processes, especially if personal clarity and empowerment have not been attributes that we have typically experienced. Imagine you are working through a dense fog and the only things you can see are the images - often hazy - of things right in front of you. If you are used to walking in this type of a fog, you learn to adapt until the fog becomes normal and expected. The only things that exist for you are the things within your vision. Yet when the dazzling sunlight breaks through the fog, suddenly you can see things you didn't know existed within your proximity as well as at a distance. So it is with discernment.

Often we limit ourselves and make choices based on only those options that we can see, options which may be placed in our line of sight by others. Discernment is the sunlight that provides us with clearer vision so that we may part the mists and see clearly both the implications of the choices right in front of us and the possibilities that we had not previously considered. As has been mentioned previously, wheat is a symbol sacred to Demeter and Persephone and one that is incorporated into the Eleusinian Mysteries. Just as one must separate the wheat from the chaff, we too must separate what is possible from the illusions of our limitations.

To be sovereign is to practice self-determination; that is, to react consciously and choose with intent. This sounds easier in theory than it often is in practice. It is not enough to be able to discern effectively, we must be willing to act on our clarity as well.

Giving our power away can be seductive, often in subtle ways. It is as though our lives are a dance. Often times, this dance is made up of movements, painstakingly choreographed by others or by our own shadows and fears about what is acceptable as well as the implications of failure. It is a general expectation for many of us that we will stick to the choreography presented to us. In many cases, if we have not given ourselves permission or learned how to act from a place of personal power, we will hold tight to this choreography even when the moves feel stiff, false, or painful. This discomfort is felt to be more manageable than the pain of what could happen if we were to consider other movements, other possibilities.

Yet, within this dance there are infinite possibilities. In any moment, we could choose to move in any number of ways. Listening to our hearts, our instincts, and perhaps our higher self, we can improvise and move in a way that flows and frees us. We can lose ourselves in the music that perhaps only we can hear and we can transform the dance into one that makes our hearts sing and brings us joy. The risks of this are significant, however, as it requires vulnerability and courage. Improvisation can be beautiful, but it can also be messy and we are bound to make mistakes and missteps from time to time. We may also find that the people around us may not be supportive of our decisions, particularly if they are used to sticking to the choreography of their own lives and/or if they had a part (intentionally or not) in choreographing ours.

Of course, we can't always control the situations in our lives and despite our best efforts we may find ourselves in positions where we feel helpless and/or victimized. It is important for us to be gentle with ourselves when these things occur. As Persephone illustrates in the more empowering versions of her myth, we can still be sovereign even when others have, for the moment, stolen our freedom to choose what happens to us. Despite being seen as helpless and incapable by those around her, Persephone refuses to see herself that way. She denies the illusion that only two choices exist for her, and she finds a third option that better serves her and those she cares about. She does not allow her pain to weaken her; rather, she uses it to grow and evolve. Finally, she stands strong and takes accountability for her decision and embraces the destiny that she has chosen for herself.

We, too, can express our sovereignty in how we choose to react and respond to what has occurred as well as in how we choose to move forward. We can enact our personal power by alchemizing our wounds and our pain to make us even stronger and more powerful (Woodfield, 2017). We can honor our personal power by both taking responsibility for how we react to our circumstances while also treating ourselves with compassion and love. To succeed in this, we must be able to part the mists, make our way through the fog and to see with clarity ourselves, our power, and the wide spectrum of possibilities that we may not have considered. With Persephone as our guide and ally, we develop our skill of discernment.

Intentional discernment takes practice. It requires that we constantly question the assumptions and limitations that have been imposed upon us and/or that we have imposed upon ourselves. We must ask difficult questions and allow our minds to explore every possibility that exists when we are faced with a challenging situation or decision. We must then attempt to keep an open mind and suspend judgement as we follow every thread of every possibility to its possible outcomes. Doing so will typically broaden the spectrum of opportunities and choices available to us, helping us to determine which path to take when we are at a crossroads or to find a "third way" as Persephone did by eating the pomegranate seeds. Strengthening our discernment can also strengthen our intuition and vice versa.

There are some techniques that we can use to develop our skill of discernment. First, just as Persephone spends one third of the year in the stillness and darkness of the Underworld, we often benefit from taking our own time - alone and in silence if possible - to rest, reflect, go within, imagine, and integrate all that we have learned. This may not always be possible in large chunks of time, but even spending five minutes in solitude and/ or meditation in the morning can greatly help us to improve our clarity. If it is truly impossible for you to go to a quiet place to meditate, consider using time in the shower or bath as you get ready in the morning as your chance to reflect and turn your attention inward.

Ask those around you that you trust for their perception of a book you have both read, a movie you have both seen, and/ or a situation that you have both observed. Doing this helps you to see the divergent yet valid perspectives and possibilities that exist that you may not have considered. Keeping a clear quartz crystal nearby can also be helpful when you need to get clarity about a situation. You can scry with the crystal or you can simply hold the crystal in your hand and ask for guidance. You may want to consider charging the crystal with an intent of experiencing discernment and receiving guidance. The information you receive may be in the form of a vision, a knowing, an auditory experience or symbolism from something you read or see in nature. Try not to have any preconceived notions about what you will experience and be sure to note any observations, symbols, and/or intuitive thoughts/experiences as a result of your work with the quartz crystal. Looking back at your journal entries over time may also provide insights.

The divination technique below can also help you to gain clarity when it comes to making a choice and/or trying to find a different path than the ones you have been presented with. Bay leaves are associated with purification and were said to be chewed by the Pythia at the Oracle of Delphi as part of their process for sharing prophecies.

Discernment Divination Technique

Materials Needed:

Cauldron or other fireproof bowl

1-3 dry bay leaves

Permanent marker (Laundry markers work well)

Lighter

Be sure to clear the space you are working in before you begin. Call on Persephone to aid you as you try to get clarity about the situation at end and which path to take. While you are focused on visualizing and thinking about the first path that is open to you in this situation, write the number one on the leafy portion of the plant to the left of the stem that goes through the middle of the leaf. Then, focus on visualizing and thinking about the second path that is open to you in this situation and write the number two on the leafy portion of the plant to the right of the stem. When you are ready, light the bay leaf at the top in the very middle or at the stem on the bottom. Pay attention to which side of the leaf takes the longest to burn.

The number on the side of the leaf that takes the longest to burn is the option that will best serve you at this time. (Note: The entire leaf my not burn the first time you light it. You can choose to stop at one lighting or continue to light until the leaf is completely burned though the latter is not necessary). Be sure to take your time scrying as the embers move along the leaf and take note of any symbols that you see. You may also want to scry in the smoke from the leaf, and note the movements and/or sounds that it makes as well.

If you are unsure if there is another unknown path that you should be considering, you can write the number one on one bay leaf, the number two on another bay leaf and leave the third bay leaf blank. Follow the same process as you did before by concentrating on the options each time you hold one of the leaves in your hand. Be sure to do this for all three leaves. Either light the leaves all at the same time or place them into an already lit fire. When the fire dies down, the leaf that takes the longest to burn or is the most intact is the option that will best serve you at this time.

If you wish to get more clarity about a "third way", cast a circle around you and formally ask for Persephone's guidance. Listen to trance drumming as you clear your mind, leaving it open for discernment. Think about the situation at hand and its implications. When you are ready to receive guidance, take one bay leaf and holding it gently in your hand over the cauldron, recite the following words:

Queen of the Underworld and Spring, Persephone
I ask that you share your guidance and discernment with me
So that I may gain greater clarity
Help me find another way
That will not lead me astray
Help me see the path that will best serve me
And the greater good - So mote it be

Place the bay leaf in an already lit fire. Be sure to pay close attention to any symbols or pictures you see both in the embers as they move along the leaf, the fire itself, and in the smoke rising from the fire. Make note of what you see as well as anything you hear and any guidance that you receive using any of your other senses. You may also journey to visit Persephone at a later time and ask her to provide you with more information about what the symbols mean. You may also try researching the symbols if you are unsure how to decipher them. If you feel that you need more clarity, you may repeat this bay leaf burning technique two more times within the current lunar cycle.

Journal Questions
- Write about your experiences with the discernment

divination technique(s). What did you see? What did you learn and/or what guidance did you receive?

- What was the most difficult aspect of the divination technique(s) for you? What came the most naturally?
- In what areas of your life have you noticed that you need the most clarity? Looking back on your past, is there a pattern? (For example, do you find that you lack discernment most with relationships? Vocational matters?)
- Why do you think you have challenges with discernment and clarity in the areas noted in the previous journal question?
- Where in your life do you feel that clarity and discernment come most naturally to you? Why do you think this is?
- Have there been any instances in your life when, like Persephone, you were able to come up with a creative solution or choice despite being given limited options? What circumstances and/or personal attributes do you think facilitated this accomplishment?

Chapter 6

Rituals for Persephone

Below are two rituals for connecting with Persephone and accessing her wisdom as part of reclaiming your personal power. These are separated into a ritual for the dark half of the year and a ritual for the light half of the year. Though pennyroyal tea is referenced in research related to the Eleusinian Mysteries, I do not recommend drinking it unless you have consulted with a medical professional as pennyroyal can have detrimental side effects, particularly if you are pregnant. For that reason, I have substituted mint tea in the ritual for the dark half.

The basket represents the "Cista Mystica" that was used during the Eleusinian Mysteries which held ritual tools and items and, according to some historians, also contained snakes. The representation of the snake is a symbol of shedding one's skin and can be a picture, a clay figure, a piece of jewelry or any other item with a snake-like appearance or energy. The representation of the pig or sow in the ritual for the light half of the year recalls the association of pigs with both the Eleusinian Mysteries and the rites of the Thesmophoria as symbols of abundance, vitality, and fertility.

The purpose of the ritual for the dark half of the year is to let go of those shadow aspects that you no longer need, much as if you were clearing a space in your garden for new growth. For this reason, the circle is cast counter-clockwise as it is this energy that is typically associated with release. Yet, the evocations move from East to North to symbolize a descent into the Underworld.

The ritual for the light half of the year focuses on harvesting the seeds you planted in the dark half and reclaiming your personal power. The circle in the Light Half ritual is cast clockwise to represent the energy of increase and growth. The evocations move from North to East to symbolize ascent from the Underworld. The evocations themselves reflect the qualities that Persephone shares with us as we walk our path to sovereignty. You are free to use different words for the evocations should you so desire.

I personally like to include on my altar a representation of the two major goddesses associated with Persephone - Demeter and Hecate. A sheaf of wheat is a simple representation that can be used for Demeter and Hecate can easily be represented by a key or a skull. However, including these representations on your altar for the rituals below is optional.

Separating the Wheat from the Chaff- A Ritual for the Dark Half of the Year

Materials Needed:

3-4 sheafs of wheat with the chaff attached (you can typically find this at your local craft store)

A small basket (a lidded basket is preferred but not necessary)

One or more dried flowers as an offering

3-4 ribbons

Small bowl of holy water

Persephone incense (see Chapter 7 for recipe)

Cauldron or other fire proof container and a charcoal disk

A representation of a snake

Permanent marker

Candle anointed with Persephone oil (see Chapter 7 for recipe)

Offering for Persephone (some examples include barley, pomegranate/pomegranate seeds, grapes, figs, olive oil, honey, wine, sweet cakes)

Any ritual tools you intend to use (i.e. athame, wand)

Mint tea

Preparation: Place any ritual tools, ribbons, and the representation of the snake in the small basket on the altar. Light the candle and the incense. Anoint yourself with the consecrated water.

Starting in the North, cast a circle counter-clockwise three times around using your hand, an athame or a wand. Start the first casting of the circle from high above you and imagine with each of the two subsequent castings that the energy is spiraling down as if you were descending a staircase.

Drink some of the mint tea and, as you do so, focus on clearing your mind and becoming centered.

Standing in the East, speak the following words:

"Hail, Persephone!
Your reappearance on Earth as flowers bloom and life returns
Provides us with perpetual hope and the promise of renewal"
Standing in the South, speak the following words:
"Hail Persephone!
You show us the power of passion and love
To enlighten, to foster strength, and to claim that which we
    desire"
Standing in the West, speak the following words:
"Hail Persephone!
You remind us that we are all born and reborn
Again and again, like the sheaf of wheat and the ear of corn
In the watery womb that connects us to the sea of Source"
Standing in the North, speak the following words:
"Hail Persephone!
As Queen of the Underworld, you teach us
To nurture the potential and treasure that often lies
Buried deep within us"
Standing in the center of the circle, speak the following words:
"Hail Persephone!
Through the endless cycle of death and rebirth
You encourage us to claim and wear proudly
The Crown of our Sovereignty"

Sitting in the center of the circle, place the sheaves of wheat before you. Concentrate on that which you most need to let go of in order to manifest the life that you desire. These may include labels that came up for you in the guided meditation in Chapter Three. Once you have identified the top 3-4 things that you need to let go of this coming cycle, use the permanent marker to write or draw a symbol for each of these on the chaff of wheat (one word or symbol per piece of wheat).

Concentrating on each shadow aspect you are sacrificing, remove the chaff from the wheat as you state the following:

"_____ you have fulfilled your purpose and you no longer serve me. I release you."

Set the pieces of chaff aside to be buried or burned after the ritual is done.

Holding the seeds in your hand, think about what it is you wish to plant to fill the void of what you just released. When you are ready, hold each seed up and state what it represents. Finally, determine the energies or qualities that you will work with to encourage the growth of the seeds. For example, if you have let go of scarcity and intend to plant abundance in its place, you might choose to foster growth by seeking new employment. Or you might choose to take an elemental approach and work with the energy of the Earth element. You could also choose to work with a quality such as gratitude as a way to help these new seeds grow.

Assign a ribbon to each energy or quality and state out loud what each ribbon symbolizes just as you did with the seeds. Tie each ribbon to the bottom of the sheafs of wheat, creating a "bouquet". Turned upside down, this bouquet forms a broom which can energetically sweep away negative energy or obstacles that may arise in our pursuit of your goals. This bouquet of wheat will remain on your altar to be used in the ritual for the light half of the year.

Starting in the center of the circle, release each of the quarters by thanking Persephone for her wisdom and guidance. When you have thanked Persephone at each of the quarters, take down the circle in a threefold, clockwise motion, starting at the bottom of the circle and moving your way up as if ascending a staircase. Gather the energy up and direct it towards the bouquet of wheat on your altar, releasing it in this manner.

When you are done with the ritual and have grounded, leave the offerings for Persephone outside somewhere and either burn or bury the chaffs of wheat. You may choose to plant the seeds literally so that there is physical representation of growth come spring. If you do not have the greenest of thumbs or you live in a climate that can pose challenges for plant growth, I recommend not doing this as I have found that if the plant dies we tend to associate that with failure, both literally and metaphorically. If you do choose to plant the seeds, I would recommend selecting plants that are hardy and easy to grow. Otherwise, you may choose to leave the seeds on your altar or carry the seeds with you in a small bag as a talisman.

Rebirth and Renewal-A Ritual for the Light Half of the Year

Materials Needed:

The bouquet of wheat that you created in the Dark Half ritual

A small basket (a lidded basket is preferred but not necessary)

Fresh flowers in a vase as an offering

Small bowl of water

Persephone incense (see Chapter 7 for recipe)

Cauldron or other fire proof container and a charcoal disk

A representation of a pig

Candle anointed with Persephone oil (see Chapter 7 for recipe)

Offering for Persephone (some examples include barley,

pomegranate/pomegranate seeds, grapes, figs, olive oil, honey, wine, sweet cakes)

An item you have created to represent your sovereign self-manifested in the light half as a result of the seeds you planted in the dark half. Examples include but are not limited to be a poppet, a piece of art, a collage, written work, a piece of music, handcrafted jewelry, or a crystal grid

Any ritual tools you intend to use (i.e. athame, wand)

Preparation: Place any ritual tools and the representation of the pig in the small basket on the altar. Light the candle and the incense. Anoint yourself with the consecrated water.

Starting in the East, cast a circle clockwise three times around using your hand, an athame or a wand. Start the first casting of the circle from near the ground and imagine with each of the two subsequent castings that the energy is spiraling upwards.

Standing in the North, speak the following words:

"Hail Persephone!

As Queen of the Underworld, you have taught me

To nurture the potential and treasure that lies

Buried deep within me"

Standing in the West, speak the following words:

"Hail Persephone!

You have reminded me that I am born and reborn

Again and again, like the sheaf of wheat and the ear of corn

In the watery womb that connects me to the sea of Source"

Standing in the South, speak the following words:

"Hail Persephone!

You have shown me the power of passion and love-including love of self

To enlighten, to foster strength, and to claim that which I desire"

Standing in the East, speak the following words:

"Hail, Persephone!
Your reappearance on Earth as flowers bloom and life returns
Provides me with perpetual hope and the promise of renewal
As I manifest that which I desire"
Standing in the center of the circle, speak the following words:
"Hail Persephone!
Through the endless cycle of death and rebirth
You have helped me to claim and wear proudly
The Crown of my Sovereignty"
Chant "Crown of Sovereignty" three times or more (See Chapter 7 for the words to the chant)

Take the bouquet of wheat off the altar and untie the ribbons, one by one. As you do so, imagine the energies that they represent increasing and integrating into your being. When all of the ribbons have been united, set the wheat aside and direct the energy you have gathered to the representation of your sovereign self on the altar. When you are done, place the representation in front of you and follow the guided meditation below.

Guided Meditation - Claiming the Crown

Sit in a comfortable position and close your eyes. Pay close attention to your breathing. Breathe in and out slowly for a few cycles until you are ready to begin. In your mind's eye, you see a door in front of you. This could be any type of door...a large wooden door, a glass door, even a portal. When you are ready, step through the door.

You find yourself standing in front of a palace in the dark of night. Standing by the entrance are two sentries. A man with dark curly hair and a mischievous smile stands on the threshold of the entrance. You approach the man and he holds out his hand. You reach into the pockets of the clothes you are wearing and place in his hands an offering. Quietly, he steps aside and motions for you to enter. You do so and the man leads you down a long hallway. The walls of the hallway are decorated with richly woven tapestries depicting scenes from Greek mythology. Finally, you arrive at a large door, fashioned from gold and set with gleaming a variety of precious gems. The man nods at you and then leaves.

You place your hand on the door and slowly push it open. You step over the threshold and the door shuts behind you. You find yourself looking down a long pathway leading to a throne. The room is dimly lit by torches lining the walls. On either side of the pathway leading to the throne are long, rectangular pools of water. You slowly make your way down the path until you arrive at the path's end. You can see that it is Persephone sitting in the throne but you are separated from her by what appears to be a stream.

You stand before Persephone and share with her what it is you wish to manifest in yourself and your life with the power of sovereignty bestowed upon you. Persephone looks deep in your eyes and holding your gaze firmly states, "No one can bestow sovereignty upon you. You must claim it for yourself". She steps away and motions towards the stream. An altar emerges from the water.

You find you carry your representation of your personal sovereignty with you. You think for a moment of all you have to gain by claiming your crown. You also think with some hesitancy of what you have to lose, what you must be willing to let go. After some time, you place your representation upon the altar, knowing that this will signal to the universe both your desire to fulfill your potential as well as your willingness to be accountable for your sovereignty.

Persephone sits back down on the throne and you watch as the altar with your offering slowly descends back into the water. As it does, you feel as though you have shed a layer of energy. You may feel vulnerable and exposed and you are unsure of what will happen next. As the altar is finally swallowed fully by the stream, a golden light emerges from underwater and you see something rising from its depths. As it reaches the surface, you see that before you is an intricate box. Light emanates from inside of it. You reach towards the box and open it. Inside the box is your crown of sovereignty.

This crown is uniquely yours - no one else has anything like it.

Take a moment to look at your crown. What is it made of? Is it large? Delicate? Is it inset with vividly colored crystals or does it have a beautiful simplicity? As you touch it, you notice that it vibrates to your touch. What does this vibration feel like? How does the crown reflect who you are at your core? In what ways does it resemble your unique personal power?

For a moment, you wait for someone to place the crown on your head but you ultimately realize that the only person with the authority to grant you the power of sovereignty is you. You gently remove the crown from the box and place it upon your head. As you do so, you feel a surge of energy rush through you. The energy is powerful, the embodiment of who you are at your most sovereign. You rise, and as you do so, Persephone rises as well. A bridge appears across the stream and you make your way towards Persephone. She tells you that you will need to attend to your crown and your sovereignty with conscious intent from this point forward in order for it to retain its power.

"In order to be treated like a Queen", she says, "You must hold yourself like a Queen. You must know your value and honor your worth in thought and deed. Though you may at times forget to wear your crown, it will never be fully lost to you."

You thank her for her guidance and provide her with an offering. You walk back along the path and through the golden doorway, holding your head high. The crown feels a bit heavy on your head at first, but slowly integration occurs until you no longer feel the crown though you know it is still there. You may your way to the entrance to the palace and when you are ready, you walk back through the door that brought you here. Take a few moments to return your attention to your breathing and when you are feeling grounded, open your eyes. If you find that you need more grounding and/or do not feel like you have fully returned, place your hands on the ground for a bit and/or eat a snack. When you have fully grounded, take some time to record in your journal what was shared with you and what you experienced.

Starting in the center of the circle, release each of the quarters by thanking Persephone for her wisdom and guidance. When you have thanked Persephone at each of the quarters, take down the circle in a threefold, counter-clockwise motion, starting at the top of the circle and moving your way down as if descending a staircase with the energy ultimately being released into the ground.

Chapter Seven

Forging the Path: Additional Methods for Connecting with Persephone

Other Names or Titles for Persephone:

Kore

Similar deities:

Proserpina (Rome), Despoina (an older Arcadian chthonic goddess said to be the daughter of Demeter and Poseidon)

Family Tree:

Mother - Demeter

Father - Zeus

Grandmother - Gaia

Uncle/Husband - Hades

Lessons:

Independence, Growth, Sovereignty, Discernment, Letting go of that which no longer serves us, Death and Rebirth, Self Determination, Speaking one's truth, Authenticity

Archetypes:

Wounded Child, Martyr, Sovereignty Queen, Psychopomp

Roles:

Catalyst for regeneration (as the Goddess of Spring)

Psychopomp and Nurturer of the Dead (as the Queen of the Underworld)

Sacred Sites:

In Greece - Eleusis, Kerameikos Cemetery in Athens, the Nekromanteion on the Acheron River in Epirus, Attica, near the River Ilissos in Athens, Nysian Plain in Boetia. Also, caves, rivers, oceans, springs, and mountaintops

Trees:

Pomegranate, Willow, Myrtle, Poplar

Herbs:

Pennyroyal, Mint, Laurel

Flowers:

Narcissus, Rose, Jasmine, Poppies, dried flowers

Crops:

Wheat, corn, barley, figs

Other food offerings:

Honey, Sweet Cakes

Stones/Crystals:

As Queen of the Underworld- Garnet, Smoky Quartz, Onyx, Ruby, Red or Orange Carnelian; As Goddess of Spring-Amethyst, Aura Quartz (typically in pinks, reds, and rainbow/clear), Blue Chalcedony, Celestite, Rose Quartz

Colors:

As Queen of the Underworld-Red (especially dark red), Black, Dark Purple

As Goddess of Spring-White, Pink, Light Blue

Animals:

Pig, Snake, Skylark, Falcon, Owl

Holy Days/Times:

Samhain, Ostara (Spring Equinox)

The Lesser Mysteries were conducted in what we know as February or March whereas the Greater Mysteries were conducted in September.

Types of Magick:

Fertility, Growth, Releasing, Shadow Work, Self Love, Self Confidence, Clarity, Grief, Connecting with Ancestors, Divination

Elements:

As Queen of the Underworld - Water

As Goddess of Spring - Air

Types of Music:

As Queen of the Underworld -Violins, Drums, Dirges

As Goddess of Spring - Flutes, Choral Music

Tarot Correspondences:
    As Queen of the Underworld: Death, the High Priestess
    As Goddess of Spring - The World, Page of Cups

Chants

"Claiming the Crown"
Nurtured by Demeter
With Hecate's wisdom you grow
Enlightened by Hades' love
Death and Birth the seeds you sow
Goddess of Above and Below
Goddess of Sovereignty
Through your lessons, I reclaim my crown
Hail Persephone! Hail Persephone!

"Descent and Ascent"
Down, down again
Into the Underworld I descend
Sifting through the shadows of my inner night
So that I may emerge, reborn in the light
Rise, rise, rise again
Rising up to the sun, I ascend
Reaping the harvest of the seeds I've sown
Through the cycle of life I have grown

"Above and Below"
Up, up above
With the light and the love
Of your mother, here
Your mother, here
Down, down below
Where the souls must all go
With your lover, dear
Your lover, dear

Eat the seeds, and you must stay
One third down below, two thirds in the light of day
Persephone, Persephone
Help me find my way

Below are recipes for incense/bath tea and anointing oil. Be sure to use essential oils as opposed to fragrance oils which do not contain the same energies and can be irritating to skin. Because essential oils can also be a skin irritant for some, I recommend only using a small amount of bath tea and/or anointing oil on skin or in baths to start to see how your skin reacts.

Persephone Incense/Bath Tea

Roses have magickal properties traditionally associated with love, purification, emotional healing, and forgiveness. As we work with Persephone and release that which no longer serves us, we may find ourselves critical of choices we have made. Rose's ability to aid in self-forgiveness combined with the healing power of water can be very effective and calming as we do any kind of shadow work.

Jasmine is also associated with love and has strong anti-anxiety properties. Whereas rose has more of a light energy, jasmine evokes an energy that is more earthy and sensual. Hibiscus is also known for its association with love as well as for assisting with freedom and independence. Bay laurel was said to have been used by the Pythia at Delphi to aid in intuition and divination. In addition, bay laurel is a good ally when one is working on release, transformation, purification, and trying to build confidence.

Patchouli is known for being very earthy and grounding, and can help with one's work in discernment. Like rose essential oil, patchouli oil was initially associated with wealth and prosperity. Just as the wealth of Greece was believed to be stored in the Underworld of Hades; so too our greatest treasures are often hidden in our shadows. This incense/bath tea is a powerful aid in transformation as we work to let go of our illusions and demons, strive to love and accept ourselves more fully, and gain the confidence to enact our personal power.

Ingredients:

2 parts dried red roses or rosebuds

1 part jasmine flowers

1 part dried hibiscus flowers

1 bay leaf, crumbled

½ to 1 part patchouli

½ of a dried pomegranate peel, crushed into small pieces or powder

7-10 drops of rose absolute essential oil

3-4 drops of patchouli essential oil

If flowers are whole, crush them in a mortar and pestle. Mix all herbs, flowers, and the pomegranate peel together in a plastic bowl with a non-metal utensil. Add rose absolute and patchouli essential oils and mix well. Place on a lit charcoal disk to use as incense. To use as a bath tea, place a small portion of the mixture in a muslin bag and allow it to sit under the faucet of your bathtub while you are running a bath so that the water runs over it.

Persephone Anointing Oil

This anointing oil captures both the dark and the light aspects of Persephone. Not only do the magickal and medical properties of the oils in this recipe support one's efforts to identify and enact personal power, they also align symbolically with Persephone and her myth.

Rose essential oil has the highest frequency and vibration of any essential oil, which is fitting as we attempt to raise our own vibration and step into our power. Like Persephone, rose oil may seem like a gentle, "light" oil but it is also a very powerful energy that can sometimes be taken for granted. Patchouli's heavy, earthy and grounding energy is appropriate for representing Persephone in her role as the Queen of the Underworld. Its association with prosperity aligns well with Persephone's quest to discover her own value and fulfill her potential.

In addition to the properties mentioned in the Incense/ Bath Tea recipe, jasmine is most commonly known as a night blooming flower. Persephone was able to blossom in the darkness of the Underworld; thus, jasmine aligns strongly with Persephone's lessons and the work of reclaiming one's sovereignty. Pomegranate oil, in addition to being great for one's skin, is known for its ability to protect the heart. On a metaphysical level, this energy can be very soothing as we work through descent and what can be a very challenging emotional time. Pomegranate oil also offers us a direct connection to Persephone and her myth.

Materials:
Dark colored glass bottle with dropper top
A carrier oil such as olive oil, grapeseed oil or almond oil
15-20 drops of pomegranate seed oil
10-15 drops of rose absolute essential oil
10 drops of jasmine essential oil
3-5 drops of patchouli essential oil

Fill the glass bottle ¾ of the way full with the carrier oil. Add the pomegranate seed oil and the essential oils. Secure the lid firmly on the bottle and shake vigorously. This oil can be used to anoint candles, worn on skin, worn in aromatherapy jewelry, added to a diffuser, and/or added to baths.

Persephone's Seeds of Wisdom

Similar to runes, Persephone's Seeds of Wisdom can provide guidance and act as a divinatory tool. They are simple to make and easy to use, and the methods for using them are versatile enough to utilize when you don't have much time. The pomegranate has long been believed to aid in divination. The Seeds of Wisdom divination technique uses physical representations of pomegranate seeds, shadows, and growth to help one discern the nature of a particular challenge or life lesson as well as identify what illusions may be blocking our path and what aspects of our personal strength we are being called upon to recognize and utilize.

The red marbles represent pomegranate seeds and symbolize positive traits and/or guidance to help you embrace your sovereignty. The black marbles represent the shadow aspect of the Underworld. This could include potential obstacles, shadow work that needs to be done, things to be aware of, and labels that you identified earlier on in this process which no longer serve you or align with who you are. The clear or green marbles represent aspects of our lives where potential fruits can be reaped from working through Persephone's lessons and enacting your personal power.

Materials:
> A bag of red marbles with flat backs (Like the kind used for planting. The larger, the better)
> A bag of black marbles
> A bag of marbles that are clear or green
> Permanent markers (Gold or silver tends to show up best on the darker colors. Gold or black tends to work best on the lighter colors.)
> A bag or box to keep the "Seeds of Wisdom" in when not in use.

1) Create three lists containing a minimum of 10 short phrases or words each. The first category will contain words that reflect major aspects of one's life. These are the areas where outcomes may occur and where the fruits of our labor can be reaped. The second category will contain words that reflect positive attributes. These

may be attributes that we already have, strengths that Persephone exhibits through her lessons and her myth, and/or general positive traits.

The final category will contain words that reflect negative attributes. The positive and negative attributes should be opposites of each other, mirroring the other attribute. For example, if one of your negative attributes is "fear", the opposite positive attribute would be "love" or "courage". If there are specific traits related to shadow issues that you know have played a prominent role in your life, you may want to start listing these first and then think of their opposites as opposed to the other way around. The major aspects category does not have to align with the other two categories in any way. In fact, it's better if you approach the major aspect category as being completely separate from the other two.

Examples are given below.

MAJOR ASPECTS	POSITIVE ATTRIBUTES	NEGATIVE ATTRIBUTES
Relationships	Trust	Illusion or Dishonesty
Career	Adaptability	Rigidity
Finances	Love or Faith	Fear
Health	Resilience	Stubborn
Spirituality	Self-Care	No Boundaries

2) Once you have all of your words and short phrases, write these or symbols to represent these with gold permanent marker on the glass marbles. Positive attributes should be written on the red

marbles and negative attributes or shadow issues will be written on the black marbles. The clear or green marbles will contain the symbols or words from your major aspects category. Leave three clear or green marbles blank to represent the unknown. These sets of marbles will be your "seeds" of wisdom.

3) Separate the seeds so that there is one pile of red marbles, one pile of black marbles, and yet another pile of clear or green marbles. You may want to place each set of seeds into a separate bag or cup.

4) Hold your hands over the seeds and say the following:
Persephone, Goddess of Spring
Queen of the Underworld
Help me explore my darkness
Let these seeds be your light
So that I may see clearly
And discern what must be done
In order to manifest a fertile harvest
From the seeds of my desires
(Note: You can use your own call to Persephone in place of the one above).

You may want to leave the seeds on an altar dedicated to Persephone for a time before or using them and/or in between use. You can also charge the seeds by the sun or the moon

Divination Instructions: Divide the space where you will be laying the marbles into three quadrants. For the left hand quadrant, you will be randomly pulling a clear or green marble to denote what area of your life has come to the forefront most recently and/or is an area for you to pay close attention to. (Alternatively, if you wish to ask a specific question about an aspect of your life, you may select the marble which best represents this aspect and place it in the left quadrant.)

In the middle quadrant, randomly pull and place three black

marbles. Seeds reflecting negative attributes represent coping mechanisms or labels in your life that are no longer serving you and are creating obstacles to success. These "seeds" can also reflect shadow issues that you need to explore in more depth.

In the right hand quadrant, randomly pull and place three red marbles. These seeds represent skills and abilities that you already possess and/or can build on which will help you to overcome obstacles and attain your goal.

If you pull the blank seed(s), this indicates that there are too many unknown variables to be able to provide direction and you should try the reading again in a couple of days.

If you lack time, you can simply pull one seed from the entire combined set of marbles to help you answer a specific question or provide information about the energies and/or suggested focus for that particular day.

Alternate Method for Creating a Simple Set of Persephone's Seeds of Wisdom

If the method above doesn't appeal to you and/or feels too complicated, you can make a much simpler set of seeds to work with. Simply take one set of marbles (any color) and write words, phrases and/or symbols on the marbles representing actions you can take.

Some examples include "patience", "initiative", "let go", "movement", "self-care", "set boundaries", "learn more", and "turn back". To use this set, simply pull a seed whenever you are feeling stuck and need guidance.

Chapter Eight

Persephone's Feast

Food can be a powerful way of connecting with deities and their culture. The Greek pantheon is unique as compared to some other pantheons in that food plays an important role in Greek myths and the functions of Greek gods and goddesses. Many Greek myths mention nectar and ambrosia which are usually considered food to be consumed only by the gods. A number of Greek deities oversee or are associated with food and drink as part of their function. Persephone is well known for her association with the pomegranate, but there are other examples as well. Demeter, as one example, is associated with wheat, corn and bread. Dionysus is said to have invented wine and is strongly associated with this beverage.

The recipes below all incorporate either foods sacred to Persephone or foods that have a Greek flavor. *Recipes contributed by Steven Corak*

Greek Summer Salad

Ingredients:

Spring Greens mix

Spinach

Arugula

1 cup pine nuts

½ cup pomegranate seeds

1 cup blackberries

8 oz Manchego, shaved (Manchego is a Spanish cheese that can typically be found at grocery stores or specialty shops)

Pomegranate Vinaigrette (see recipe below)

Mix all of the greens together. Toss the mixed greens with the

Pomegranate Vinaigrette. Top the salad with the berries, nuts, and cheese.

Pomegranate Vinaigrette

Ingredients:

5 tbsp pomegranate seeds, juiced

5 tbsp vegetable oil

3 tbsp apple cider vinegar

1 tsp stone ground mustard

1 tbsp of shallot, minced

2 tbsp brown sugar

½ tsp lemon juice

Combine all ingredients except the vegetable oil. Slowly drizzle in the oil while stirring vigorously to emulsify.

Pomegranate Chicken and Kale

Ingredients:

1 lb goat cheese

¼ cup heavy cream

¾ cup pistachios, finely chopped

2 ½ tbsp honey

1 head of kale

1 lemon peel

½ tsp chili flakes

4 chicken breasts

2 lbs red potatoes, quartered

1 sprig rosemary, chopped

Salt

Pepper

½ Pomegranate Reduction (see recipe below)

Bring a pot of salted water with chili flakes and lemon peel to a boil. Blanch the kale and immediately transfer it to an ice bath.

Drain and cool kale.

Combine goat cheese, pistachios, and honey in a mixing bowl and gently fold in heavy cream until smooth. Season with salt to taste, and then cool.

Season chicken breasts with salt and pepper and bake at 400 degrees until they reach an internal temperature of 165 degrees. Rub potatoes in olive oil and season them with salt and pepper to taste. Top with rosemary and roast along with the chicken for approximately 20 minutes. Be sure to check on them every so often to ensure that they don't get overcooked as cooking times can vary.

Spread goat cheese mixture across plate and place kale on top of the cheese. Slice chicken breasts and lay over the kale. Drizzle pomegranate reduction sauce over the chicken. Plate with the roasted red potatoes.

Pomegranate Reduction

Ingredients:

2 ½ cups pomegranate seeds, juiced

1 ½ cup sugar

1 cup honey

2 cinnamon sticks

1 tbsp orange zest

1 tbsp lemon zest

1 tsp salt

3 cups water

Combine all ingredients and bring to a boil. Reduce to a simmer until mixture is thick and has a syrup like consistency. Remove cinnamon sticks. Set aside half of the reduction if you are going to be making Persephone's Pastries as well.

Persephone's Pastries

Ingredients:

3 eggs

1 ½ cups flour

3 tbsp olive oil

Pinch of salt

¾ cups toasted walnuts, chopped

1 bag chocolate chips, melted

½ of the Pomegranate Reduction sauce prepared for the chicken

Combine flour, eggs, olive oil, and salt to form a dough. Knead for 5 minutes. Roll dough into thin sheets and cut into strips that can be rolled into a loose cigar shape. Transfer to a batch of frying oil at 350 degrees and fry until crispy and golden brown. Transfer to paper towel to remove excess oil. While still warm, toss the pastry in the pomegranate reduction. Dip ¾ of each pastry in the melted chocolate to coat and sprinkle with chopped walnuts.

Conclusion

We all have unique gifts and talents that no one else can offer the world in the same way that we can. Often, we keep these talents locked away and we give away our power in ways both big and small. This typically happens without our full awareness and unless we are willing to actively apply Persephone's lessons to our lives, this abdication will happen again and again, ultimately stifling our ability to fulfill our potential and manifest the life which we truly wish to live. By giving our power away and being afraid to share our unique talents and perspectives with others, we do a disservice to the deities that we worship and the world around us.

If Persephone teaches us anything, it is that we must be willing to delve into our own inner Underworld in order to be liberated and find joy in the Spring of our rebirth. There is strength in vulnerability, and there are vast treasures waiting to be found in the darkness. While we don't know for sure what happened during the Eleusinian Mysteries, historians and others who have researched these rituals agree that initiates felt much less fearful of death after they had undergone the rites of the Lesser and Greater Mysteries. Initiates were reported to have achieved a peace of mind that had previously eluded them.

You, too, have the ability to let go of the fears that have held you back and severe ties with the things that no longer serve you. When we come face to face with that which we fear, we begin to see its illusory nature and learn its true purpose so that we can use our shadow wounds, our fears and our pain to nurture our growth much like the rich soil nurtures growth in the darkness of the ground below us. Persephone's lessons require difficult and sometimes terrifying inner work. Yet this work is necessary if we are to wield our personal power and experience greater happiness and autonomy.

As you undertake this work, you may experience resistance from those close to you, particularly if they haven't been willing or able to confront their own shadows and heal past wounds. This can be an incredibly difficult issue to deal with but know that by connecting with and utilizing your personal power you give others permission and courage to do the same. Just like Persephone had to choose to live her own life rather than submit to the demands of those she cared for, we too must choose to speak our truth and live our lives on our own terms if we are to achieve our full potential.

There are many ways in which you can incorporate your work with Persephone in your spiritual practice. These include but are not limited to:

- Answering the journal questions in the earlier chapters of this book
- Looking back and reviewing past journal entries and reflecting on the progress and/or changes that have occurred
- Making an altar dedicated to Persephone
- Anointing a candle to Persephone with the Persephone Oil from Chapter 7 and lighting the candle for a bit each day as you sit at your altar
- Meditating on Persephone's lessons
- Visiting Persephone and her sacred sites in meditation
- Reading various versions of Persephone's story
- Chanting for 5-10 minutes each day using one of the chants in Chapter 7 or your own chants

If you are interested in a deeper, ongoing connection you might also consider working with her psychopomp aspect by volunteering at a hospice or exploring her aspect as Goddess of Spring by planting and maintaining a garden.

If the darkness gets to be too much, just remember that you

have a guide and a willing light in the darkness in the form of Persephone. If the shadows of doubt are speaking too loudly to ignore and you are having a hard time believing in yourself, take comfort in Persephone's transformation from a vulnerable, powerless victim to a mature, confident Queen, ruling not only herself but an entire realm. Like Persephone, you too have the ability to enact your personal power and claim your own crown of sovereignty.

Journal Questions

- With what aspect of Persephone do you resonate most? Why do you think this is?
- What have you learned about yourself throughout this journey with Persephone?
- You should now have a clearer vision about who you are and what you desire? How would your life be different if you were acting from a place of pure authenticity and claiming what you want? What would a typical day look like? How would you feel?
- Persephone's lessons embody the enactment of personal power. In what areas of your life would you like to more effectively enact your own personal power? What small changes can you make over the next month and year to align yourself with this vision? What big change(s) will you need to make?
- While Persephone ultimately had to make the decision that was best for her, throughout her myth she is surrounded by people who care about her. Who, in your life, can you count on to be a sounding board and/or provide support?
- Who, in your life, cares about you but may be inadvertently expressing their concern for you in a way that is not supportive of your sovereignty? What are some ways you can address this issue? What boundaries do you need to create?

- Take a look at the suggestions for connecting with Persephone on a daily basis. Which suggestions resonate with you? What additional ideas do you have? Pick one idea to incorporate into your daily practice for the next lunar cycle. You may want to keep a journal to record your experiences with this practice.
- Look back at your journal entries for questions starting with Chapter One. What have you learned throughout this journey? How have your perceptions and/or beliefs changed?

References

Blackthorn, Amy. *Botanical Magic: The Green Witch's Guide to Essential Oils for Spellcraft, Ritual, and Healing.* (Canada: Weiser Books, 2018)

Brannen, Cyndi. "Life Lessons from Persephone, Queen of Pain" April 8, 2018. https://www.patheos.com/blogs/keepingherkeys/2018/04/life-lessons-from-persephone-queen-of-pain/

Campbell, Joseph. *The Power of Myth* (New York: Doubleday, 1988)

Campbell, Joseph. *Transformations of Myth Through Time* (New York: Harper and Row, 1990)

"Goddess Archetype: Persephone" 2004, http://goddess-power.com/persephone.htm

Jenkins, John Phillip. "LSD" September 24, 2018, https://www.britannica.com/science/LSD

Farrar, Janet and Bone, Gavin. *Lifting the Veil: A Witches' Guide to Trance Prophecy, Drawing Down the Moon, and Ecstatic Ritual* (Portland, OR: Acorn Guild Press, 2016)

Parca, Maryline and Tzanetou, Angeliki, eds. *Finding Persephone: Women's Rituals in the Ancient Mediterranean* (Bloomington, IN: Indiana University Press, 2007)

Preka-Alexandri, Kalliope. *Eleusis* (Athens: Ministry of Culture Archaeological Receipts Fund, 1997).

Reif, Jennifer. *Mysteries of Demeter: Rebirth of the Pagan Way* (York Beach, ME: Samuel Weiser Inc., 1999)

Serena Mirto, Maria. *Death in the Greek World: From Homer to the Classical Age* (Norman, OK: University of Oklahoma Press, 2012)

Shelmerdine, Susan C. *The Homeric Hymns* (Newburyport, ME: Focus Publishing, 1995)

Shinoda Bolen M.D, Jean. *Crossing to Avalon: A Woman's Midlife*

Pilgrimage. (New York: Harper Collins, 1994)

Shinoda Bolen M.D., Jean. *Goddesses in Every Woman: A New Psychology of Women.* (New York: Harper Perennial, 1984)

Stehle, Eva. "Thesmophoria and Eleusinian Mysteries: The Fascination of Women's Secret Ritual. In *Finding Persephone: Women's Rituals in the Ancient Mediterranean,* edited by Maryline Parca and Angeliki Tzanetou (Bloomington, IN: Indiana University Press, 2007)

Spretnak, Charlene. *Lost Goddesses of Early Greece: A Collection of Pre-Hellenic Myths* (Boston, MA: Beacon Press, 1992)

"Thesmophoria". *Encyclopedia Britannica* https://www.britannica.com/topic/Thesmophoria

Uzzell, Jennifer. "Eleusinian Mysteries". In *Seven Ages of the Goddess,* edited by Trevor Greenfield (Washington: Moon Books, 2017)

MOON BOOKS

PAGANISM & SHAMANISM

What is Paganism? A religion, a spirituality, an alternative belief system, nature worship? You can find support for all these definitions (and many more) in dictionaries, encyclopaedias, and text books of religion, but subscribe to any one and the truth will evade you. Above all Paganism is a creative pursuit, an encounter with reality, an exploration of meaning and an expression of the soul. Druids, Heathens, Wiccans and others, all contribute their insights and literary riches to the Pagan tradition. Moon Books invites you to begin or to deepen your own encounter, right here, right now.

If you have enjoyed this book, why not tell other readers by posting a review on your preferred book site.

Recent bestsellers from Moon Books are:

Journey to the Dark Goddess
How to Return to Your Soul
Jane Meredith
Discover the powerful secrets of the Dark Goddess and
transform your depression, grief and pain into healing
and integration.
Paperback: 978-1-84694-677-6 ebook: 978-1-78099-223-5

Shamanic Reiki
Expanded Ways of Working with Universal Life Force Energy
Llyn Roberts, Robert Levy
Shamanism and Reiki are each powerful ways of healing; together,
their power multiplies. *Shamanic Reiki* introduces techniques to
help healers and Reiki practitioners tap ancient healing wisdom.
Paperback: 978-1-84694-037-8 ebook: 978-1-84694-650-9

Pagan Portals – The Awen Alone
Walking the Path of the Solitary Druid
Joanna van der Hoeven
An introductory guide for the solitary Druid, *The Awen Alone* will
accompany you as you explore, and seek out your own place
within the natural world.
Paperback: 978-1-78279-547-6 ebook: 978-1-78279-546-9

A Kitchen Witch's World of Magical Herbs & Plants
Rachel Patterson
A journey into the magical world of herbs and plants, filled with
magical uses, folklore, history and practical magic. By popular
writer, blogger and kitchen witch, Tansy Firedragon.
Paperback: 978-1-78279-621-3 ebook: 978-1-78279-620-6

Medicine for the Soul
The Complete Book of Shamanic Healing
Ross Heaven
All you will ever need to know about shamanic healing and how to
become your own shaman...
Paperback: 978-1-78099-419-2 ebook: 978-1-78099-420-8

Shaman Pathways – The Druid Shaman
Exploring the Celtic Otherworld
Danu Forest
A practical guide to Celtic shamanism with exercises and
techniques as well as traditional lore for exploring the Celtic
Otherworld.
Paperback: 978-1-78099-615-8 ebook: 978-1-78099-616-5

Traditional Witchcraft for the Woods and Forests
A Witch's Guide to the Woodland with Guided Meditations and
Pathworking
Mélusine Draco
A Witch's guide to walking alone in the woods, with guided
meditations and pathworking.
Paperback: 978-1-84694-803-9 ebook: 978-1-84694-804-6

Wild Earth, Wild Soul
A Manual for an Ecstatic Culture
Bill Pfeiffer
Imagine a nature-based culture so alive and so connected,
spreading like wildfire. This book is the first flame...
Paperback: 978-1-78099-187-0 ebook: 978-1-78099-188-7

Naming the Goddess

Trevor Greenfield

Naming the Goddess is written by over eighty adherents and scholars of Goddess and Goddess Spirituality.

Paperback: 978-1-78279-476-9 ebook: 978-1-78279-475-2

Shapeshifting into Higher Consciousness

Heal and Transform Yourself and Our World with Ancient Shamanic and Modern Methods

Llyn Roberts

Ancient and modern methods that you can use every day to transform yourself and make a positive difference in the world.

Paperback: 978-1-84694-843-5 ebook: 978-1-84694-844-2

Readers of ebooks can buy or view any of these bestsellers by clicking on the live link in the title. Most titles are published in paperback and as an ebook. Paperbacks are available in traditional bookshops. Both print and ebook formats are available online.

Find more titles and sign up to our readers' newsletter at
http://www.johnhuntpublishing.com/paganism
Follow us on Facebook at https://www.facebook.com/MoonBooks
and Twitter at https://twitter.com/MoonBooksJHP